JOHN WAYNE,

MY FATHER

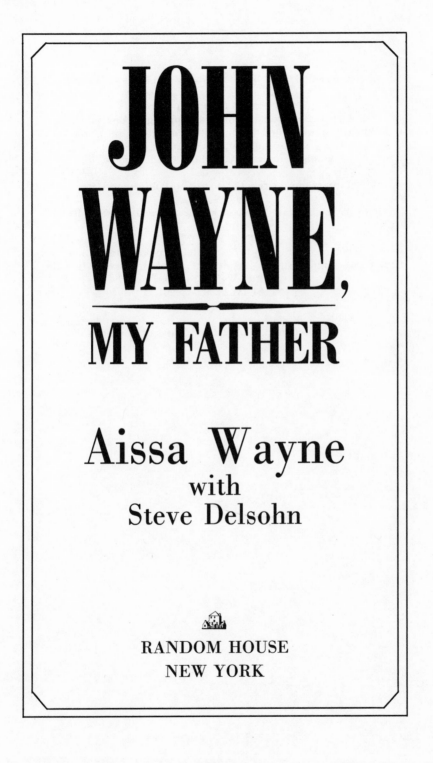

JOHN WAYNE, MY FATHER

Aissa Wayne
with
Steve Delsohn

RANDOM HOUSE
NEW YORK

Library of Congress Cataloging-in-Publication Data
Wayne, Aissa.
John Wayne, my father / Aissa Wayne, Steve Delsohn. — 1st ed.
p. cm.
ISBN 0-394-58708-1
1. Wayne, John, 1907–1979. 2. Motion picture actors and
actresses—United States—Biography. I. Delsohn, Steve. II. Title.
PN2287.W454W38 1992
791.43′028′092—dc20
[B]   90-52881

Manufactured in the United States of America
98765432
First Edition

To my mother, Pilar Wayne,
the most gracious human being
I have ever encountered.

—Aissa Wayne

To my father, Norman Delsohn

—Steve Delsohn

ACKNOWLEDGMENTS

My thanks to my three beautiful children—Jennifer, Nicky and Anastasia—for their special love and also for once in a while tucking *me* in at night! Thanks to Mary St. John and Debbie Schweickert for reliving part of the past with me. Thanks to Lou Nelson, Frank Weimann, and David Rosenthal for their enthusiasm and support. And a special thanks to Steve Delsohn for being so extraordinarily sensitive and understanding.

—Aissa Wayne

My thanks to Mary St. John, Pilar Wayne, and Debbie Doner for sharing their lives and insights; to Lou Nelson and Cheryl Booth for their energetic and expert contributions; to Frank Weimann for his unstinting belief in the book and in me; to Joni Evans for her support and generous spirit.

A special thanks goes to David Rosenthal, my kind and extraordinary editor.

Thanks to my wife, Mary Kay, the best friend I've ever had and forever the love of my life.

—Steve Delsohn

JOHN
WAYNE,
MY FATHER

PROLOGUE

I am staring up at him in the cool delicious darkness of a theater, my father etched sixty feet high on a white-silver screen. My girlfriend nudges me. I pass our candy without shifting my gaze from the screen. It is 1963, I am seven years old, and today is a rare occasion. Almost always I see my father's movies at home, in our projection room, with my mom and dad and our new baby, Ethan, and sometimes my father's movie star friends.

Unless I am with my parents, or at school, I do not leave the house much at all. We live in Encino, in the San Fernando Valley, and our white colonial house sits at the top of a steep mountain rise, high above five rolling acres, all enclosed by ten-foot walls. At the bottom of our twisting driveway is a camera, fixed on our tall electric gate. Though sometimes we call it "the compound," our estate is lovely as well as confining, precisely what my parents desire. They are frightened I might get kidnapped, especially my mother, who comes from Peru, but knows about the evil that can descend on Hollywood's children.

Today I am free. It is Saturday, late afternoon, and I am sitting in a theater with my girlfriend and her mother, surrounded by anonymous people. Up on the screen my father makes a joke, not even a joke, just a stoic remark, but it's in his familiar drawl and the smiling strangers around me murmur their approval. I feel a trace of pride and a pinch of resentment, that all these faceless people think my father is such a charming man.

The movie is over and I'm glad. It's another Western, and I'm a little sick of them. My eyes still set for blackness, on the street I am blinded by sunlight, and the sticky summer air curls my golden brown hair. On the ride home my girlfriend and her mother discuss my dad and the movie. They are animated, and I know by their glances they want me to join in, but I just don't. Like my father I am prone to silent moods. Politely saying good-bye, I watch their shrinking car leaving our driveway, wondering if I should have asked them in, to see my father, and if they are mad, and whether the whole ride home they'll talk behind my back. I am not all that paranoid—I don't think—but sometimes I can't tell who likes me only for me.

He isn't home anyway. My dad is again working late this weekend, over the mountain pass in the peculiar place called Hollywood. Usually, when my father is in town, he's always home for dinner. The second he bursts in our front door, he always says, "HELLO THE HOUSE!" He *booms* it, and the air in our house crackles with his energy. Then I run down the stairs and jump off the last one, into my father's outstretched arms. I am not as little as I once was, but it hasn't stopped our ritual. We've been doing it for years, and no one else is invited.

Tonight my father misses dinner, and there is no "hello the house." Tonight he's in my room before I can climb off my bed to greet him. Inside my bedroom, my father is a giant in a dollhouse. When he sits on my bed now, it sags and groans under his weight. I need to know why he's so late, want to tell him how striking he looked on the full-size screen, but I don't get the chance—my father wraps me in his arms and pulls me to his chest. I can smell his Camel cigarettes, his Neutrogena soap and Listerine. I start feeling edgy. My father always talks before he hugs.

When my dad releases me, he cups my chin in his hand. I am lost for a moment inside his ice-blue eyes. My father has the bluest, lightest eyes I have ever seen.

"Aissa?"

There is a tightness to his voice. Now I know something is wrong. All I say is, "Yes, Daddy?"

"Aissa, when you get older, and realize I'm not as strong as you think I am, will you still love me?"

"Yes, Daddy."

Always with my father, it is "Yes, Daddy"; by now I say it out of reflex. Really, though, I am puzzled. My father is the strongest man on earth. At seven years old I do not know everything, but this I know utterly and positively. I want to ask why he'd say something so silly, but now he is looking outside my window and just that quickly I lose my nerve. Maybe my dad is only tired. Maybe his violent smoker's cough will not let him think straight.

As he always does when he is in town, my father curls the bottom of my blanket under my feet and leans back in to kiss me goodnight. He holds me close again, then I shut my eyes and pretend to be sleepy. I peek at his broad back as he leaves, then lie unsettled in darkness for what seems like hours. The following morning, and for many days after, his strange words echo again and again through my mind.

Sipping bitter coffee in a chilled hotel room, I stare outside at a listless Western morning. It is June 11, 1979, and the doctors say today will be the day. Today my father will die of cancer.

I do not weep. Instead I feel frozen, pinned here in my

chair by grief and memory. It's ironic, I suppose, that my relationship with my movie star father has somehow played out in three stages. Or, as it is said in Hollywood, three acts.

When I was a little girl, I looked at him through idolatrous eyes. I saw only the good and pretended about the rest. Around the time I turned six, my fear of my father set in, and I was intimidated by him for more than ten years. What we had between us began transforming again when I was nearing eighteen. As I started asserting some independence, as my father was losing his health and also losing my mother—and began turning more and more to me—most of my fear of him dissolved. For so many years, my real words had gone away whenever my father and I had gotten alone. And then, I could finally talk to my father.

Now I am twenty-three, and he and I have never been closer. I hate that it took so long, but I believe I am finally seeing him clearly. My father is vast, endearing, courageous, caring, tenacious, and vital. Still, he is not the faultless hero who strode through my early childhood. He has deep fears of his own. He has demons, self-doubt, and towering rage. John Wayne is not invincible, and soon he will not be around to protect me.

Over the years, learning the truth about him has been stunning. At times, it has thrown my entire childhood into question: Was it ever really what I once believed it to be? Was he?

Still, learning the truth has also made me love my father harder, the father who exists, not the image we once both created, then clung to so fiercely together for so many years. Even more than I once loved that dream, I love my real father with all his imperfections. I want him to know this. More than anything in the world I want him to know. But today my father will leave me, and now our time has run out.

I am not writing this book as a love letter to my father. Neither am I intent on destroying his public image, as some

Hollywood children have done to their parents. When my father was still alive I was constantly asked by the press, "What is it like to be John Wayne's daughter? How does it feel?" I never knew how to succinctly respond to such a complex subject, so mostly I issued stock answers. In the past several years, my own three children have started to ask me: "What was our grandfather like? What was John Wayne like?" For my kids, but also for my own cathartic reasons, I wanted to put down on paper the life I shared with my father.

When I was eight weeks old, my father turned forty-nine. He was nearly sixty when I was ten. I viewed him through my own childhood lens: the notion that he'd been scarred and shaped by events I knew nothing about rarely crossed my mind. He was a grown-up. He sat at the head of our table. I figured his story pretty much started there.

I've done some looking into his past in order to come to grips with myself and with my dad, and to understand where John Wayne was in his life when he fathered me.

1

The year was 1953. Truce had been reached in Korea, and if that peace was uneasy, the country nevertheless was not at war. Bumper stickers announced I LIKE IKE, and trust ran high for the reassuring first-year president. Still a youthful medium, television had superceded radio and already had motion pictures reeling. One of TV's new, top-rated programs, *Ozzie and Harriet,* and many other shows like it, painted a placid picture: American home lives free of complication.

It was illusion. In Hollywood, where illusion was manufactured, no one knew this better than John Wayne. That fall, my father was wrapped in domestic scandal.

In November 1954, he would marry my mother, Pilar,

and his third and final marriage would endure for the next two decades. In 1956 my parents would have me.

But now, in late October 1953, his second marriage was ending, wildly, and reporters tripped over each other to detail the sordid news. The gossip mavens gushed, and even the restrained *Los Angeles Times* called it "The steamy divorce trial of the towering screen actor John Wayne." All the while the public was enrapt. In 1950s Hollywood, the public images of private hell-raisers—and back then that included my dad—were honed, shined, and sanitized to keep negative press at a minimum. Still, there is no hiding hostile divorce, not when it's John Wayne's, and the trial for my dad was an embarrassing mark on a soaring career.

My father was then forty-six, already had twenty-five years in the business. After a long, arduous climb to the top of his profession, he was finally box office gold. In 1951, producer Howard Hughes had paid him $301,000 to star in *Flying Leathernecks,* and this was called the highest one-film salary ever given to an actor. Between 1948 and 1953 my hard-working father starred in fifteen films, most notably *Fort Apache, Red River, Sands of Iwo Jima, Rio Grande,* and *The Quiet Man.* His role in *Sands of Iwo Jima,* as Marine Sergeant John M. Stryker, won him more than an Oscar nomination; it had stunning impact on people who saw it. When my father charged up Iwo Jima Hill, only to be cut down by sniper fire just steps from the top, people wept in their seats. Their tears did not go unnoted by the czars ruling Hollywood. With the film industry ailing, its income and stature diminished by the rise of TV, the power brokers came to view my dad as a rare and critical asset. "There's nothing wrong with Hollywood," a producer told *Cosmopolitan,* "that a dozen John Waynes couldn't cure."

Privately, what needed fixing was his second marriage. Back in 1944, his first marriage, to Josephine Saenz, the mother of his first four children, had ended in divorce. My father remarried in 1946. He met his next wife in Mexico, a country he loved second only to this one. On the night Ray

Milland introduced my father to Esperanza Bauer, who called herself Chata, she claimed to be a part-time actress. In truth, Chata was a dark, voluptuous, high-priced call girl. By the time my father discovered the facts of her life, he'd fallen in love.

Not surprisingly, my father never spoke to me about Chata. I never heard about her until after he died, and at first I was shocked and disbelieving. But then I learned more. Evidently, Chata told my father she desperately sought a new life, to escape her past and marry a man she loved. I also learned that my father's first marriage, to Josephine, had had little physical contact its last several years, and that Chata Bauer was blatantly sexual. At that stage of his life, perhaps Chata was who my father needed. Besides, he said he loved her, and when John Wayne fell in love he tended to marry. Those who knew him well always called my father "the marrying kind."

Nevertheless, when he brought Chata back to the States and later wed her in Long Beach, his close friends said he was making a dire mistake. John Ford, the director my father most often worked with, came down harder, shunning my dad for nearly two years. By then the lives and careers of Ford and my father were tightly linked, and my dad once told me that Ford was the only man he had ever feared. An expert manipulator of actors, Ford's machinations often continued offscreen. But he never swayed my father as much as their mutual fans believe, for my father was simply too willful. And Ford's hostility notwithstanding, my father and Chata set out to make their unlikely marriage work.

They could and then they couldn't. For the seven stormy years they stayed married they separated numerous times. When the marriage finally shattered, the allegations made for a lurid trial. Too much angry suspicion, too much hard liquor, and not enough fidelity—these were the mutual charges.

According to my father's testimony, Chata's mother had quickly moved in with the newlyweds, and he would often come home to find drunken wife and in-law, entwined in each other's arms, lying out cold on a bed. Chata, he also testified, once threatened to kill him.

During the making of *Angel and the Badman,* Chata had convinced herself that my father was sleeping with Gail Russell. My father's handpicked costar, Miss Russell was then twenty-three, emotionally fragile, and dazzlingly beautiful. My father told the court that on the evening of the movie's wrap party, when he arrived home at one-thirty A.M., "My wife refused to let me in. I could hear her and her mother talking about me loudly. I rang the bell but they wouldn't open the door. Then I broke a glass panel, reached in, and opened it myself. Chata and her mother, they came charging out. Chata had a forty-five in her hand. She and her mother were fighting over it."

Under oath, Chata said she thought my father was a burglar; that's why she ran out clutching the gun. My father told a different story. He said his wife had been drunk and hysterical, demanding to know if he'd just come from a motel with Gail Russell. Insisting he betrayed her, she turned the loaded pistol on him, threatening to end her husband's life. When his attorney asked my father if there had been any affair with Miss Russell, and a trip to any motel, my father said, "Absolutely not." He said he and Miss Russell had shared only friendship.

By the end of the week, Chata had accused my father of twenty-two acts of physical cruelty, repeating again and again that John Wayne had "clobbered" her. My father had sworn he never struck his wife, just protected himself from her boozy rages, and he countered with thirty-one charges of his own. A girl waved an enormous sign on the jammed steps of the courthouse: JOHN WAYNE, YOU CAN CLOBBER ME ANY TIME YOU WANT.

When it became clear how grotesque things were becoming, both sides opted to settle. The trial ended abruptly, after three days in Superior Court. The judge intervened, granting the Waynes an uncommon divorce, reserved for California cases where neither party concedes the other's charges. If they chose, in one year both could remarry. In the interim, my father retained his Encino estate. He agreed to pay Chata $150,000, all her current debts, and $50,000 per year for the next six years.

No one claimed victory. Only the lawyers escaped un-bloodied.

Chata died late the following year in a Mexico City hotel room, thirty-eight and an alcoholic. The newspapers said she died alone, of a heart attack. Her sad little room was strewn with empty bottles.

My father, who had once loved her, did not ride off into the sunset. He did not live happily ever after.

But he did find a deeper love.

In 1952, his marriage to Chata without hope and the lawyers preparing for court, my father flew to South America. He was scouting locations for *The Alamo,* an epic Western he one day intended to act in, produce, and direct. When he arrived in Peru, my father was told to look up Richard Weldy, who worked for Pan American Airways when he wasn't leading tours up the waters of the Amazon. Though he never planned it, Richard Weldy also led John Wayne to his future wife.

Weldy took my dad to the small jungle town of Tingo Maria, where a Peruvian film crew was squarely in the midst of shooting a scene. By the time of their arrival the afternoon sun was dying. By firelight, a young Latin actress danced barefoot for the camera, her long hair dark and unruly, her legs thin and sculpted. This was the vision that charmed my father the first time he saw my mother.

In a photo taken moments after they met, my mother's flowered dress is cut to fall off one milky white shoulder. Her full red lips and exotic dark eyes are aimed up and at my father, whose shirttail hangs out. His hair is cut boyishly short, and his massive left hand dwarfs what is likely a cock-tail. His downward gaze on my mother is fixed like a laser.

She must have been an interesting girl. The daughter of a Peruvian senator, Pilar Palette had been expected to marry a Latin aristocrat. As a child, her Catholic mother had used God and religion as bludgeons, filling her small daughter's head with scorched and anguished images of hell, where little Pilar would truly be damned and burn should she fail to toe her mother's concrete line. After the death of her father, my mother finally rebelled. She didn't marry a Latin blue blood, but Richard Weldy, the raucous Irish-American.

On the fateful day he led my father to Tingo Maria, Weldy and my mom were already estranged. He wanted her back, so Weldy showed up with John Wayne, a famous American film star. My mother was duly impressed, but not by Weldy. When my father sought to charm, few could resist him. He was more than tall, handsome, wealthy, and famous. He had that stride, that voice. The moment she met him my mother said she was smitten.

But Richard Weldy had eyes. He took my mother aside and told her he needed her back. My mother wanted to scream. Weldy had cheated on her; she'd discovered it and been crushed. While she wondered where John Wayne had slipped off to, my mother told Weldy the marriage was over. When she asked if he'd started divorce proceedings, Weldy said no and stalked off.

Under an inky sky, that night my parents shared dinner. With the cast and crew around they were hardly alone, and yet they felt that they were. My mother was nervous, my father patient. He was forty-five, she was barely twenty. She stood five feet three inches tall and weighed at most 100 pounds. A grizzly bear of a man, six feet four and 230 pounds, he must have seemed twice her size. Unaware that his first two wives had also been Latin, my mom was surprised at his knowledge of Latin custom. In fractured English, my mother told him he'd been wonderful in *For Whom the Bell Tolls*. My dad grinned his lopsided grin and explained that she must mean his pal Gary Cooper. In their first intimacy, he took her delicate hands in his own and my mother blushed. Too soon the dinner was ending. My father stood up and said, "I guess this is good-bye."

My mom went to bed feeling flushed, vaguely aware she had suffered a loss. My father went to his own room, leaving the next day at first light.

My dad was deeply superstitious. He bellowed whenever he saw a hat on a bed. For a man who once had been a poor boy, this was not bad luck but disaster—a hat on a bed meant no work. On rare rainy days in Southern California, my mother preferred opening her umbrella before she stepped outside, and my dad would see her and cringe. When my parents played poker, and a playing card turned face up, its owner had to stand and circle his or her chair three times. At dinner, my father never let anyone hand him the salt. Instead we had to place the salt on the table. If anyone handed my father the salt, he said they'd be passing him their bad luck.

Believing as he did in fate, perhaps my father was not amazed to find himself face-to-face with my mother again, this time back in America. As my parents always told it, it happened on a Monday, just a few months after they'd met in Tingo Maria. Scared but excited, my mom had been flown from Lima to Hollywood, to Warner Brothers studios, to dub some dialogue for the movie she'd made in Peru. At the end of her grueling first day, she started for the stage door. As she leaned on its bulky frame, the door opened up from the opposite side.

It was pushed by my father.

Two years later they married.

When my parents ventured into Hollywood, it was not only my dad who commanded attention. My Peruvian mother was not only stunning, she was uncommon, and this multiplied her appeal. One day at Warner Brothers, Marlon Brando was crouched over a commissary table, checking out John Wayne and the young woman sitting with him at a table across the room. Though my father respected his talent, he and Brando weren't friends. Once John Ford wanted Brando and my dad for a potential film, and Ford asked my father to approach him. When my father called, Brando said, "Who is going to direct?" and my father said "John Ford." Brando said, "He's not my kind of director." My father didn't belabor it—that was never his style—and neither man filled the silence. From that point on they were only acquaintances.

Now Marlon Brando was eyeing my mother. Maybe he didn't hear they'd recently been married, perhaps he had and didn't care. Brando was barely thirty, gorgeous and arrogant, sizzling with success after coming off *The Wild One* and *On the Waterfront.* Brando sent over a friend to ask John Wayne if Marlon Brando could meet his alluring companion.

My father said one word: "No!"

That evening at home, my dad went into a jealous rage. It was my mom's first glimpse of his dark side. She realized, only then, that my father was not the characters he played on the screen, men who did not just have self-assurance, they reeked of it. He was more complicated than that, and more conflicted. He was driven by pride, but also by insecurity, and a troubled past he could never completely take flight from.

2

M y father was born on May 26, 1907, in Winterset, an Iowa town of less than 3,000 residents. His parents were Mary and Clyde Morrison, both Anglo-Saxon protestants. A football player in college, Clyde was muscular, quietly amusing, easygoing, and quick to trust others. He was a druggist, of Scottish, English, and Irish descent. Pure Irish, Mary had blue eyes and red hair. Vivacious, intelligent, ambitious, she dominated her husband and son.

When my father was born during their first year of marriage, his parents named him Marion Michael Morrison. When Marion turned five, his parents bore a second son named Robert. It was then that my father's life flipped upside down.

His mother chose her youngest boy to shower with love, saving only what trickly drops remained for my father. My dad resented his mom, even while aching for her love. Perhaps the rejection he felt as a child later influenced the unsettling way my father behaved toward me—lavishing me with affection, demanding my constant reassurance that I loved him back. Perhaps, after all those years, he was still trying to fill a void that cast such painful shadows over his childhood.

Night after night, my father's parents fought bitterly. Mary was a perfectionist, Clyde a romantic and dreamer. While my father listened, his mother berated his dad, usually beginning with his lack for making money and his overwillingness to extend his customers credit, then spilling into all the other ways he had left her disappointed. Mary often threatened to leave her husband, stopping only when Clyde fell ill and began coughing blood. Clyde had tuberculosis, and a doctor said he would die if he remained in Iowa. The Morrisons moved westward in 1915, to the dry heat of Palmdale, California.

I doubt if they knew what they were getting into. At the desolate edge of the Mojave desert, with its hot, bone-dry winds, the Morrison's new home had no gas, electricity, or running water. As my father once told a writer, their rural property teemed with reptiles and rodents. "I don't mean just a few," my father said. "Seems to me like there musta been millions. The more you killed, the more they kept on comin'." My dad had recurring nightmares, about greasy rattlesnakes cornering him as he tried to scream out. As the snakes crept through his subconscious, my father would sweat and moan in the desert night.

Despite the harshness of the new land, Clyde was determined to homestead. He grew corn in the desert and actually had one plentiful harvest. The volatile market plunged, though, and the family barely earned enough to buy food. Mary branded her husband a failure. She doted more and more blatantly on Robert, leaving my father embittered, feeling unloved by the most important woman in his life.

He found no refuge at school. Rising at five A.M., he walked four miles to his classroom, all the while dreading what awaited him. Tall for his age and still exceedingly thin, he also spoke with an accent his California schoolmates had never heard. My father was ridiculed, especially for his name, which he despised. The older boys called Marion "little girl." They asked him why he wore pants instead of a skirt. I think one of the reasons my father frequently acted so macho in later life was to compensate for this boyhood torment; I believe it scarred him deeply.

For the lonely, impoverished Morrisons, one year in the Mojave desert felt like ten. In 1916 they moved west again, this time to Glendale, where Clyde went back to working at a drugstore, and where money still was short. Nine-year-old Marion acquired a second-hand bicycle. He got a paper route and delivered the *Los Angeles Examiner.* On his daily route, my father's springy-haired Airedale trotted alongside him. He had named the dog Little Duke, and that's how my father landed his world-famous nickname. Some friendly Glendale fireman, seeing my dad and his dog together day after day, started calling my father "Big Duke." Soon, it shortened to Duke. The monicker stuck, and only his mother continued calling him Marion.

One morning in eighth grade my father approached the firehouse with a gashed lip and a purple eye. He threw down their newspaper, attempting an escape without explanation, but the firemen called him over. My father confessed: he'd been attacked, again, by the same cruel bully at school. One of the firemen, a former professional boxer, taught my father to fistfight. His aggressive new skills notwithstanding, my father continued avoiding the boy, determining where he was likely to be, then going elsewhere. After school one day the boy found him. My father said he felt scared, but fought through his fear and punched the boy in the eye. Unlike so many bullies, this one did not turn and run the first time he was struck back. He and my father fought until both were sore and bloodied. As my father told the story, the boy never touched him again.

Though still slim and sensitive to slights, his confidence bloomed when he starred as a pulling guard in football at talent-laden Glendale High. While learning to drink on weekends with teammates, during the week my dad excelled at school. He wrote for his high school newspaper, joined a debate team, and became a voracious reader, a habit he would indulge the rest of his life. By senior year he was earning straight A's. Vowing to earn a college degree, which he knew his parents couldn't afford, my father applied to the U.S. Naval Academy. He thought they would pay for his education, and armed with that he could learn to be a lawyer. But my dad was rejected.

He turned back to football, and the University of Southern California, which had offered him a scholarship to play offensive line. Grabbing it, my father enrolled in pre-law. Just as he was about to go home at the end of his freshman year, he discovered his parents' marriage was ending. He was not exactly surprised, but divorce in 1920s America was hardly the commonplace it is today, and my father felt shamed and scandalized. In retreat from the two angry voices of his childhood, he distanced himself from both parents. Rather than go home and take sides, he asked his coach, Howard Jones, to help him secure a job for the summer. Jones sent my dad right to the lot at Fox, and told him to ask for Tom Mix, the cowboy star who loved USC football, and for whom Jones provided box seats for all USC home games. In return, Mix had promised Jones he'd give summer jobs to his players.

Mix took my dad to his favorite bar, where the actor and athlete got drunk. Mix promised my father *two* jobs—one as his personal trainer, one as an extra in the star's next movie. But when my father reported to work, he had a job moving furniture and props from set to set. "I was also a grip," my father used to recall. "Around the rest of the country, they call that a janitor."

One day at Fox my father spotted Tom Mix, resplendent in the red-leather backseat of a limousine, its black doors embossed with his gold initials. Reintroducing himself, my dad politely reminded Mix of their meeting. Deadpan, the actor turned away without a word, dismissing my fuming father. Perhaps this first ugly impression later had something to do with my father's disdain for industry liars and phonies. "There's some real SOB's in this business," my father used to tell me.

That summer, working as a prop man on the set of *Mother Machree,* he first encountered John Ford, thirty-one years old and already supremely gifted. In those days Ford was in the habit of hiring the USC football team as extras for his cavalry movies. My dad worked on a few, unbilled, sometimes never making the final cut. Regardless, the Fox directors saw my father on film and sensed his raw appeal. "Dammit," said the legendary director Raoul Walsh, "the son of a bitch looked like a man."

As the nation inched nearer to the Depression, my father plunged into a malaise of his own. His second year at USC, spanning 1926 and 1927, was one of life's critical junctures after which nothing is ever the same. First, he was fixed up with a girl named Carmen Saenz, but fell madly in love with her dark-haired sister Josephine (who would someday become his first wife). His sophomore year he also made varsity football, part of a celebrated team that captivated Los Angeles. That November, the season practically over, my father went bodysurfing one morning, and was pounded into the shoreline by a late-cresting wave. With his right shoulder muscle ripped, he kept going to practice all week, traumatizing the tissue even more. Though my father stayed on the roster and received his varsity letter, his shoulder would not allow him to play football. Unable to perform, my dad would lose his scholarship.

His glory days shockingly over, he sulked and received poor grades. At the end of his second semester, feeling nervous about his future, my father asked John Ford for a full-time summer job at Fox. Planning to earn enough to pay his fall tuition, my dad never returned to college. He was twenty years old, the same age I was when I left USC nearly half a century later.

At Fox my father did prop and stunt work. Rehabilitating his shoulder, he performed strenuous workouts at the old and famous Hollywood Athletic Club. Then in 1928, *Hangman's House* was released. This John Ford movie had songs and the sound effects of bells and whistles, but the actors were silent and the dialogue was in subtitles. Directed by Ford and produced by Fox, *Hangman's House* was my father's first credited role. It was also the first time John Wayne's face could clearly be seen on celluloid. He played an Irish peasant, a spectator at a horse race, who takes off his white cap at the end of a thrilling finish, busts down a white picket fence with some other fans, and sprints into the track. It was a turning point in his life. Seeing himself on-screen lifted my father out of his doldrums, gave new rise to his dreams.

For better and worse, John Wayne was hooked on making movies.

3

John Wayne Presented Daughter by Third Wife
Actor John Wayne's wife presented him with a daughter
yesterday at St. Joseph Hospital, Burbank, where both
mother and the child were reported in good condition.

—Hedda Hopper,
April 1, 1956

Duke Wayne got two hours' sleep in 48. Pilar and he got to
bed at 1 A.M. Saturday; she shook him awake at 3:30; he stayed
with her till 2:07 that afternoon, at St. Joseph's, when Aissa,
7 pounds 8 ounces, arrived. . . . Pilar was on the phone talking
to a reporter 50 minutes after her birth. . . . "Aissa means
absolutely nothing," Pilar told us. "We're calling her that
because it goes well with Wayne."

—*The Hollywood Reporter,*
April 2, 1956

I n 1950s Hollywood we were still called "show business
families," and I was a show biz baby. A cooing, flatulent,
drooling public figure on diapered display for the
flashbulbs and pens. I was a "celebrity offspring," a
now-and-future "Hollywood princess," and mine would
be a chronicled youth. My silken hair and green eyes would
grace the cover of *Cosmopolitan,* the pages of *Photoplay,*
and untold American newspaper readers saw me blubbering
my hairless pink head off in a photo that ran over the wire
service on the second day I drew breath. By then my father
was Hollywood royalty, the industry's top leading man using
gross receipts as criteria. In the photograph that ran in the
papers the day after I was born, I am cradled by a grinning,

relaxed John Wayne, the embodiment of big American dreams.

One day before, my successful father had not been so smooth. Despite having been through this white-knuckled process before—with Michael, Toni, Patrick, and Melinda, his children from his marriage to Josephine—my father wasn't prepared when my mother woke in the night and announced that her water had broken. First he botched the dash to the hospital. As usual, my father drove too fast, this time down all the wrong streets. By the time he found St. Joseph's my mother had gone into labor. It lasted through dawn and into the early afternoon. While she grunted and cried and prayed, he paced and exhorted and whistled—when my father was nervous he whistled—until finally growing so skittish he went down to greet other new babies. And so it turned out that my father was not in the room at the instant I was born. When they did usher him back in, he kissed my mother's cheek, turned to me, his swaddled infant . . . and threw a volcanic fit.

"The baby's not breathing!" he screamed. "The baby's not crying!"

The pediatrician tried explaining I was normal and healthy.

"She isn't crying, goddamn it. Babies are supposed to cry!"

He insisted I cry, demanding they prick my heel with a needle. Only when I wailed like a banshee did my father hush up and beam. Then he snatched me up in his arms, and the rest of my life I would feel my father's obsessive grip.

Everyone seeks redemption. When I was a baby, I think my father looked at me and saw a chance for his.

Through all his public success before I was born, he was haunted by private failure. After he and his first wife divorced, he was not always around to raise their four children. Though they worked with him on some movies, though he saw them every Christmas, they mostly grew up in a father-less home.

My father had married Josephine Saenz in 1933, after a lengthy courtship begun his last year at USC. Except for physical beauty, they had seemed to be opposites. The daughter of a prominent doctor, Josephine was a product of wealth and religion, most secure in the presence of socialites or priests. My father's parents had barely scraped by, and my own father was always politely indifferent to church. As a young man, I am told, my dad was earthy, hot-blooded, sex-ual. Apparently Josephine was reserved and far more chaste.

They fell in love regardless, and rapidly had four chil-dren. Legally, the marriage lasted ten years, until 1943, but they'd fallen out of love years before that. People tend to take sides in divorces, and those sympathetic to my dad have mostly laid the blame with Josephine. They say she was overly patrician, overly prudish, too intensely Catholic. My father, on the other hand, the one time he spoke of it to me, blamed only himself. Many years later, when my own parents were splitting up, my dad began confiding in me for the first time in my life. I was eighteen years old when he came into my room and said he'd never been unfaithful to my mother.

"But I destroyed my first marriage, Aissa," my father said, referring to Josephine. "I was a different man back then. I was much more selfish." He then let his voice trail off, all but confessing old infidelities.

In 1944, Josephine gave my father a divorce at his re-peated insistence. "Because of my religion," she announced in a statement to the press, "I regard divorce as a purely civil action, in no way affecting the moral status of my marriage." Josephine raised their first four children alone, instructing them in her strict Catholic ways. As for my father, he never stopped sending money to her and his older children. Until his death, he always said he was proud of Josephine for raising the kids alone and so well. He helped Michael become a film producer, relied on him to handle part of his business, and gave Patrick his first break as an actor.

As for me, my dad told me to love the older kids as brothers and sisters, not as half-brothers and -sisters. I tried to, but I never knew if their warmth was real or merely a show to placate my dad. It was all very cordial between us, and superficial. Taking our cue from our father, we never talked about real feelings, so I don't really know what they thought back then of me or my dad. Today our relationships are more comfortable, but when I was younger I barely knew my half-brothers and sisters.

Evidently, my father also felt he never knew his older children as much as he should have. Because he had not hung in there, because he had hurt their mother, my father told my mom, he always felt his other kids never truly forgave him. Although he never confessed it to me, I think he suffered tremendous guilt over this, while never shedding the grim fear that his first four kids did not love him. One day that guilt and fear would manifest itself on my brother and sister and me: my father thirsted so hard for our love, sometimes he left us no room to breathe.

Now I can better understand why. His childhood had been hurtful. So had his first attempt at having a family. Whatever blessings my father found later in life could not mend all those wounds. What made living with my father hard, and unnerving, was that he mostly suppressed what was churning inside him. To his family, he rarely expressed his inner feelings, or even admitted he had them. With all that bottled emotion, its release often came in the form of misdirected rage. Even today, I'm still surprised when other women tell me they were never scared of their fathers.

But that all came later. When I was born in 1956, my father was nearly fifty. I not only made him feel young and virile, I gave him a second chance to do right by his children. When I was an infant, my mother said my dad was not a diaper changer. In all other ways, however, she said he behaved like an "idiot father. It was a beautiful thing to watch. I've never seen a man so entranced by a child."

And I, in turn, was addicted to daddy's attention.

*

My dad was shaving in his silk pajamas. My parents both had private dressing rooms, and this morning I was in his, peeking through the mist at his image in the mirror. He always left several bars of Neutrogena soap on the brick ledge of his sauna, and they'd melted and dripped over the rocks, perfuming the wafting air with my father's sweetest smell. Wonderment in my three-year-old eyes, I just stood there and stared while he stroked the stubble from his whiskers.

I stared at my father constantly. My attraction for him—emotionally, physically, psychologically—was very, very strong. If my father was around I felt compelled to be near him, and just as intense was his need to shield me from suffering. One day, when I was six, I saw just how powerful my hold over him was.

At the Warner Brothers studio, my dad kept an old goofy bicycle, with thick tires and wide-spread handlebars. He used to ride me around on the lot while people smiled at us and waved. One day he propped me up on the handlebars and we went to visit Lee Marvin, to whom Warners had also given an office. A man appeared in our path from behind a building, my father roughly braked and I flew forward, landing heavily on my face. When my blood began trickling my father shuddered, a twitch running through his neck and shoulders. As he picked me off the concrete he looked sick to his stomach. "Oh my God," he kept frantically saying. "Oh my God, Aissa, are you okay?" The rest of the day he kept watching me and stroking my hair. In the morning, the red bruise stretched from my upper lip to cheekbone. After that we walked or drove in cars.

Like most fathers, mine was also capable of jealousy. As I am told by my family, about the time I began to utter familiar sounds, we were visited at our home by his two closest friends, John Ford and the character actor Ward Bond. I craned my neck at Mr. Bond and called him "Da da." Saying nothing, my father managed a feeble smile, and Ford and Bond both caught it. After that, my mother says, they never allowed John Wayne to forget the pained expression he wore the day his baby called another man daddy.

In those days he loved showing me off, and naturally everyone indulged him; to praise me was to praise John Wayne. But truth be told, with my green eyes and sandy hair I was a pretty little girl, but I was no knockout—for one thing, my father's big nose looked better on him than on me. Still, I quickly understood that my status carried far greater weight than my looks. While all children learn to manipulate adults, as a movie star's daughter I saw how I could take even further advantage. In the presence of my father and other grown-ups, I could get cookies, money, compliments—anything. One of Dad's friends used to press a hundred-dollar bill into my tiny pink hand the three or four times he saw me each year. At the start of adult parties, my father always carried me on his shoulders, where I was fawned on by his admirers, basking in their attention as long as they cared to heap it. Throughout my early childhood, I was told by a chorus of older voices what a cute, cute, *cute* little girl I was, and so intelligent too! And why should I disbelieve their sugary words? As long as my father stood next to me, I could not be found lacking, picked on, or threatened. Even later, no matter how afraid I ever became of my dad, the world without him was scarier.

Like many Hollywood children, my fears began at a very early age. On the surface our celebrity childhoods glowed with privilege and glitter, but sometimes the fairy tale twisted. Ever since the Lindbergh child had been abducted and murdered in 1932, threats of kidnapping and extortion were common among the famous and rich. They were rampant in Hollywood, though not always reported to the media, and there was not an industry parent who at times did not feel dread that someone was stalking his or her child. My own parents could not afford to ignore their vulnerability, and so they exerted stringent control over me.

I was not to play outside in front of our house.

I might get kidnapped.

I could never spend the night at a girlfriend's, never experience the giddiness of a slumber party.

I might get kidnapped.

Everyone knew who John Wayne's kid was. I was instructed not to talk to or glance at strangers.

I *would* get kidnapped.

This was drummed into my head, primarily by my mom, until a corner of my brain started to burn with it. Alone, I imagined gruesome scenarios: *If men in masks did come over the walls and take me away, then asked for a million dollars, would my father pay it?* I'd decide that my father would—of course he would!—but my mind would not let the matter go and my stomach would clench back up: *What if he doesn't? He always says he never has enough money. He doesn't* have *a million dollars!*

My father also warned me about the possibility of kidnapping, but not nearly as often or as vehemently as my mother. Perhaps because she was foreign born, my mother took a harder measure of Americans than my father did. Raising a movie star's daughter, in a country prone to violence, she seemed stone certain that something or someone rotten lay waiting for me Out There.

Perhaps I'd have been less afraid if our house was not at the top of a hill, or if we'd lived closer to the street or other families. As things were, I rarely woke up where I had gone to sleep. In the dead of night, I would stumble into my parents' bedroom, where I would be lulled back to sleep by my father's rhythmic snoring. My own room at night was too spooky. Outside my bedroom window stood a California pepper tree, a robust, lovely tree chock full of singing birds by day. At night, on my bedroom wall, the tree cast bony, hideous shadows. As a child I began fearing my own imagination, which turned every whistling wind, each creaking hall, into something vague and eerie.

Even during the day I often felt resentful of my physical surroundings. Not that they weren't splendid. Our house was a two-story white colonial with high pillars, allowing us a view of the whole sprawling San Fernando Valley. Winters, pomegranates and oranges hung red and orange from our private orchard. In spring, the mountain face beyond our pepper tree exploded with shiny pink moss. In the late '50s, while the rest of the Valley was building homes at a dizzying pace, the hills of Encino was still a languid, undeveloped area with numerous ranches, horses, and orchards. The only thing our estate lacked was other children for me to play with. Just as my father had been, I was a terribly lonely child.

Without other kids, our compound could feel like a prison. For days or weeks at a time, I would go off with my father to witness the world—Africa, Spain, London—then be whisked back to my oversheltered existence. Wanting to cut the odds of danger, my parents kept strict tabs on my "free" time. Mostly I played by myself, or with our four dogs, in locked isolation behind our walls and gate. Sadly, as a result, I learned to prefer the company of adults rather than other children. Emboldened by their blanket praise, I was confident and lively around adults. With other kids, I was a very different little girl. Encountering them only at school, and even then held apart by my father's fame, I often felt awkward and ill at ease.

The few girlfriends I had I rarely saw out of school, as I was not allowed to walk home with them, not even a block, when the school day ended. Instead, the schoolbus driver picked me up and dropped me off at the bottom of our driveway. For the first day or so it made me feel special. After that, what I felt was alienation. Instead of telling my parents, I characteristically kept my feelings suppressed.

Weekends were more relaxed, but still served as reminders of how different I was. Saturdays and Sundays, a man named Fausto drove me down the hill to go ice-skating. Fausto worked around our house for years; I liked him, and I always went ice-skating willingly. I loved gliding over the ice in my little skirt, and the tightness I felt from my thick socks and skates. And yet I disliked skating alone, and afterwards hardly tasted the skating rink's little pizzas. I was distracted by my envy, as I watched the chattering packs of "normal" children. As a young girl I actually dreamed of walking out my front door and playing with kids from our street. A simple dream, it would never be realized.

My favorite playmate then was still my father. When he was in town, even going to sleep had its pleasures. At night my dad was more serene, and I knew that was the time to make a play for softness. I used to say, "Daddy, help me sleep." For a man with such thick, powerful hands, my father was extremely deft. Using his fingertips, he caressed my mouth, my nose, my shutting eyes. The instant he stopped I would wiggle, until he had put his hands back on me.

I had good reason to stretch those moments. By morning, my father's gentle touch was nowhere to be found. Mornings, my dad was a slave to his energy. It was extraordinary, and it exhausted even his children. To watch my careening father attack a new day, to try and keep pace with him, was to feel very old, and very, very lazy, before our time. He never slept late. Ever. When away on location, he always rose by four-thirty or five A.M. Even at home in his own bed, his eyes popped open by dawn. Any time at all, my father hated being alone. Mornings, wired by energy and caffeine, he hated it doubly, and could not stand for others to sleep after he'd gotten up. If his family was not out of bed by seven sharp, my father woke us—with all the finesse of one of his onscreen drill sergeants.

Every morning he'd barge into my bedroom, practically shouting, "It's time to get up! It's seven o'clock in the morning! Come on!"

When I was a child this irritated me. As a teenager, often out late the night before, it became positively loathsome. I should have told my father, but never did: at that time I still feared him, and rarely told him my true feelings. Besides, had I told my father I hated the way he woke me, he would have stopped, but his feelings would have been bruised; somehow, I would have paid for it later.

I should have told him anyway, because many years later I still pay for my silence. At thirty-five, I still wake up many mornings feeling alarmed and frightened, the residue of being jarred awake throughout my childhood.

I suppose it was all part of living with a man so zealous and forceful. No matter what his mood, my father overwhelmed me. His presence was so electric, our cavernous estate felt so much fuller and safer when he was at home, that when my father left I could not forget he was gone. My earliest and most exact memory of separation comes from when I was three years old. Knowing he was leaving, again, I wouldn't stop whining and crying to my mom. "Mom, Daddy is really going. Daddy is really going."

My mother slapped my face. "Aissa," she said, "don't be ridiculous. Why do you keep going on and on? He's just leaving for a little while."

A kind of shock came over me, and the moment her hand struck my cheek I shut off my emotions. After that when my father left, I kept my longing inside.

My mother must have felt guilty and told him what happened. Because before he left for location, my dad did something new. He sat on my bed his final evening at home, dabbing away the dampness beneath my eyes. "Every night I'm gone, honey," he said, "I want you to look at the stars. Wherever I am, I'll look at them, too. And no matter how far apart we are, we'll know we've looked at the same stars."

And so I did, that and each endless night thereafter, until my father returned. I went to my window and looked at the stars, brilliant in the blackness all around, and yearned for an arm so long I could touch the lights with my finger.

4

T oo young to know it then, I realize now that my mother was under tremendous pressure during the time when she slapped me. At the end of the 1950s, the life of Mrs. John Wayne was far from picture perfect. Like me, my mother relied on him, felt secure when he was near, and could come undone when work stole him away. She also had an additional cross to bear. My Peruvian mother was still in cultural passage, adjusting to the racing pulse and swollen narcissism of Hollywood. Some of this was heady. Much of it left her displaced and insecure. Eventually, her glittering new life-style nearly cost my mother her life.

By the time we moved to Newport Beach in 1965, my father rarely attended Hollywood parties. He still saw his old

Hollywood friends—Claire Trevor, Maureen O'Hara, Dean Martin, John Ford, Henry Hathaway—but always in relaxed surroundings. When he did have to attend showy Hollywood functions, he often came home chafing, "Every one you go to, you see the same damn people, saying the same damn things. All that changes is the women's dresses." The older he became, the more my father hated flashiness. He even hounded my mother not to wear makeup. "I can't stand women who wear all that crap on their face," he would say. "A woman looks best in a pair of jeans, a white blouse, with her hair down. Pilar, why don't you go without makeup today? You know how much I love you without makeup."

Our Encino days were much different. Then, my father still went to quite a few Hollywood soirees, and even threw some himself. He primarily did it to please and impress his new wife. Looking back, their lack of communication was unmistakable—my mother often felt uneasy at these parties, too. This was the moral, I suppose, of not just my parents' marriage, but of our life as a family. Rather than having real communication, we all tried pleasing one another by pretending—and frequently wound up doing all the wrong things.

At a party one night in Encino when I was still an infant, finally my mother did not hide her emotions. Instead she blew up, and threw Robert Mitchum out of our home. It was the first night they met, but as my dad explained it all to me later, my mom resented Mitchum even before that.

According to my dad, in the early '50s he'd launched a production company, wanting more control of his own films and increased overall clout within the industry. By 1954 his company was called Batjac, and its debut film was *Blood Alley.* Eager for Batjac to charge out of the gate, my father signed three impressive talents: Lauren Bacall and Robert Mitchum to play the leads, and director William Wellman *(The High and the Mighty),* whom James Mason once characterized as a "tough little bastard." The third day of shooting, Wellman called my dad in a snit. He said Mitchum was drinking all night, sleeping through morning wakeup calls, making location life miserable for cast and crew. As producer, my father urged conciliation, but one day Mitchum stormed off the set and said he could not work for Wellman. Wellman insisted my father move into the starring role. Although my dad had once passed on the script, feeling the role needed Mitchum's devil-may-care, he finally relented and took over the part.

Later, my dad discovered that William Wellman *drove* Robert Mitchum to quit (though not necessarily to drink). The TV show *This Is Your Life* had once profiled Wellman. When the show's producers asked the acclaimed director for a list of people to interview, Wellman included Mitchum, whose stalled career Wellman had boosted in 1946 by casting Mitchum as the lead in *The Story of GI Joe.* Mitchum told the producers, no, he didn't have time to talk about William Wellman. When Wellman found out, he was livid. When the two men worked on *Blood Alley,* he took his revenge by badgering Mitchum around the clock.

At the time, my mother knew none of this back history either. All she saw was her husband packing for yet another location, for one more separation—and all because of Robert Mitchum. After *Blood Alley* came out, I imagine it was my dad and not my mom who invited Robert and Dorothy Mitchum to my parents' formal party. Dressed in a low-cut gown, my mother greeted Robert Mitchum without any rancor. He and his wife were guests in her home, and my mother intended to treat them with kindness. Unfortunately she was not paid back in kind.

"Boy," Robert Mitchum said, peering down my mother's dress, "do *you* need a new bra."

The bra was new; Mitchum had probably already started drinking. Nevertheless, my insulted mother demanded he leave that instant. The Mitchums walked out before my father had even said hello. When my mother told him why the Mitchums had gone, my father was careful not to crack the thinnest smile. As I've been told by old friends of my family, even John Wayne was wary of his new wife's toughness. It was also one of the reasons my father adored her.

Her fiestiness was so endearing, my dad may have overlooked my mother's fragility. Over the years I think we all did. In the way that husbands and children become too self-absorbed, we were blind to the anxieties my mother must have felt as a woman, a mother, a superstar's wife. My mother was strong, not unbreakable.

The facade she maintained began splintering in 1959. With very little formal education, she secretly felt inadequate around my father's gaggle of famous friends. In Peru she had never even considered meeting Hollywood glitterati; now, in her halting English, she was expected to trade witty American banter. Within her own family, my mother was torn between marriage and motherhood, between following around her globe-trotting husband and rushing back to Encino to be with me. The stresses took their toll. With fraying nerves, wilting self-esteem, and insomnia, my mother looked up a Beverly Hills physician noted among insiders for treating Hollywood wives. The man prescribed Seconals. That evening my mother slept peacefully. Within months, she was taking pills every day. To sleep. To combat depression. Before Hollywood parties. She took them then in lieu of liquor, to try and loosen up, to mask her insecurities, in the face of her husband's hard-drinking fast-track crowd.

My mother later told me what her drug addiction was like, the nightmare she went through. Even after the pills had grabbed her by the throat, she never believed she'd become addicted, never thought it could happen to her, until the day her barbiturates ran out. On location with my dad in Louisiana, she experienced the terror of drug withdrawal. Her mouth went dry. She could not take a good breath. Her heart tried exploding out of her chest. She panicked. She hallucinated. She tried slashing her wrists.

Something inside her forced her to stop, and we did not lose my mother. After my father hired a private plane and sent her home with two nurses, she woke up in a California hospital, remembering little of it. "Your father did the only thing he could," my mother told me years later. "Thank God he put me in a hospital where I could get some help. Because I did not know what was happening to me."

I was three years old at the time of the crisis, much too little to comprehend what was going on. For many years, neither my mother nor father spoke of it. Then, when I turned thirteen, my mother sat me down and told me the story, and neither of us tried choking back our tears. It was all so sad and desperate, so radically unlike the image I'd crafted of my mom. That image was strictly of a mother. I never saw her beyond that role, with a life separate from her husband and children's. I never saw her as a woman, with a unique place in the world, and a unique set of troubles.

At the time of the telling, I didn't ask too many questions. Of course I went on loving her, and my respect for my mother grew. I knew it could have been her secret, stashed in a cranny of her past. My father's PR people hushed it up, the press never found out, so there was never any danger of my reading it, or hearing it regurgitated at school. Even if my dad had been the type of man to discuss such things with his children—human frailty, human emotion—I doubt he would have told me about my mother's near-suicide. Knowing my father, he'd have rightly felt that decision belonged to her.

Why did my mother tell me? After asking myself that question and finding no answers, one day I put it to her. I was her daughter, she simply said. She felt I had a right to know.

5

Belying his black-and-white public image, in real life my dad was a warm shade of gray.

As a child he had once felt spurned by his mother. As a Hollywood star many years later, I believe he still craved love and acceptance. Unlike a Marlon Brando or Warren Beatty, John Wayne aimed to please, not to be mysterious. He gave the fans, the press, America, precisely what he knew they wanted: the Duke, a man of action and not ideas.

In fact, my father *was* a physical creature. But contrary to his simplified image—the taciturn, uneducated Westerner living on a ranch with all his horses—he also cherished art, his collection ranging from Renoir to Remington, the distinguished Western artist; greatly preferred the sea to the plains; had little affection for horses, viewing them as little more than tools of his trade; played chess compulsively; wrote and rewrote many of his own speeches; read four newspapers a day when in between movies; and read thousands of books during his lifetime.

For pure escape, my father favored mysteries: Agatha Christie, Rex Stout, and Raymond Chandler. He was also a fan of Hemingway, more as a novelist than as a man. My dad once told a close friend he considered Hemingway self-important and ostentatious. To my knowledge my father and Hemingway never met, but I do know they had at least one indirect encounter. In 1957, when Hollywood adapted *The Sun Also Rises,* a script was first sent to my father. Would he consider playing Jake Barnes, the American expatriate whose genitals had been shot off during the war? Amused, my father said, "I respect Hemingway's work, and I'm honored they want me. But do they really think I could play this part? Even if I wanted to, no one would let me."

Other than Hemingway, mysteries, and novels he thought might translate well to the screen, he stuck mostly to nonfiction: political histories, military biographies, anything at all by Winston Churchill, the public figure my father most revered. In an interview with *Playboy* in 1971, when his questioner asked him who he would most like to spend time with, my father replied, "That's easy: Winston Churchill. He's the most terrific fella of our century. He took a nearly beaten nation and kept their dignity for them. Churchill was unparalleled."

When my father spoke to me of his Hollywood peers, he also had more good words than bad. Though he never regarded them as his models or idols, he had heartfelt respect for Jimmy Stewart, Richard Burton, Spencer Tracy, and George C. Scott, whose work in *Patton* my dad singled out as a tour de force. He also praised the restrained and honest acting of Gary Cooper, and yet he never liked Cooper's *High Noon,* still widely hailed as a Western classic. My father didn't criticize Cooper's performance, but the movie's central premise. In an entire American town, only one man has the nerve to confront the bully. Any American town, my father said, would have more than one brave soul. Finding the scenario implausible, he said it undermined the whole movie.

Although he did not appear on TV until late in his life, I never heard him disparage it, or imply that its actors were any less skilled than those working in feature films. He was especially fond of Lucille Ball in *I Love Lucy,* Hal Linden in *Barney Miller,* and Jackie Gleason, both in the *Honeymooners* and *The Jackie Gleason Show.* Saturday nights in the late 1960s, at the end of each *Jackie Gleason* show, when Gleason came out and drank his coffee and smoked his cigarette, my dad always said it was the only time he really missed smoking.

When it came to his contemporaries in film, I only heard him speak once with any real venom. Gene Hackman could never appear on-screen without my father skewering his performance. I wish I could tell you why he so harshly criticized Hackman, but he never went into detail. Although it's pure speculation, had my father lived to see more of his work, I think his view of Mr. Hackman would have changed. Back then, however, my father called Hackman "the worst actor in town. He's awful."

He was also harsh toward the fabled star of *Gone With the Wind.* Clark Gable, he told me, is "extremely handsome in person. That's one guy that doesn't need Hollywood to make him look good. But Gable's an idiot. You know why Gable's an actor? It's the only thing he's smart enough to do." My dad called Gable handsome but dumb at least four or five times, and now I wonder if it had something to do with my father's friend, John Ford. During the filming of *Mogambo,* Ford and Gable had clashed again and again and the subsequent feud had simmered for years. In my father's way of thinking, disloyalty to allies, support in any fashion for their enemies, was expressly forbidden. If Clark Gable took on John Ford, my father's code demanded that John Wayne stand by his old pal.

Perhaps my father's comment—Gable acts because it's

the only thing he's smart enough to do—also pointed to his own ambivalent feelings toward actors and acting. While he always said he "loved the goddamn business," he thought of himself as more of a star than an actor. "How many times do I gotta tell you," he frequently told the press in one of his most famous quotes, "I don't act at all, I *re*act." My father explained, "In a bad picture, you see them acting all over the place. In a good picture, they react in a logical way to a situation they're in, so the audience can identify with them." He also said, "All I do is sell sincerity, and I've been selling the hell out of that since I started. . . . I was never one of the little theatre boys. That arty crowd has only surface brilliance anyway. Real art is basic emotion. If a scene is handled with simplicity—and I don't mean simple—it'll be good and the public will know it."

As Katharine Hepburn once said of him, my father had an "extraordinary gift. An unself-consciousness in front of the camera, a unique naturalness, developed by movie actors who just *happened* to become actors." Ms. Hepburn was right. My dad had dreamed of becoming a lawyer, and even after he stumbled into acting, he always eschewed Hollywood terms like "my craft," or "my motivation." Like two of his mentors, John Ford and Howard Hawks, he considered filmmaking a job, and not an art form.

My father enjoyed the money, awards, and acclaim. But working hard, simply working hard, also brought him real satisfaction. When it came to working longer and more strenuously than anyone else on a film set, he needed no director's prodding. I think it had more to do with his physical constitution than with his ego. The same life force that brought him bursting into my bedroom every morning at seven A.M. enabled him to perform at peak efficiency when exhausted actors half his age were entering scenes on wobbling legs. My father made more than 200 movies, spanning five decades. To survive that long in Hollywood, an industry that has always devoured its own, perhaps most of all a person must *keep going.* With all that adrenaline surging through him, I'm not sure my father had any choice.

As for his mixed feelings about his profession, he always said he felt honored whenever he received a script, and he said it ingenuously. I know that he loved the medium, loved movie *making.* But on some emotional level, I think he felt embarrassed to be an *actor.* George Bernard Shaw once said, "An actress is something more than a woman. An actor is something less than a man." While my father would never evaluate such a notion with me, I'm quite sure he knew the quote. And while he never castigated actresses, and respected specific male actors, male actors as a group were open season. Most Hollywood actors lacked depth, my father told me. He called them decadent, weak-willed, effeminate. Or as he said, "faggy." Being an actor himself, especially after bearing the childhood stigma of having a feminine name, could be one reason why he always seemed so hellbent on displaying his machismo. That, and his days as a singing cowboy.

In truth, my father could not sing at all, nor play the guitar. So while Hollywood dubbed it—two men would stand off-camera, one singing, one strumming—my father faked it. For a short series of 1930s B Westerns, he was reluctantly billed as a crooning cowpoke named Singin' Sandy. In those days, my father said, Hollywood cowboys were "pretty," with their snow-white Stetsons, their uncreased faces, their tender, mellifluous voices. One of his favorite stories revolved around one of his earliest casting calls. While he and another cowboy actor read lines at an audition, the manicured-looking man said, "What do you expect? I've been working all day out in the field." Stepping out of character, my father turned to the producer and director. "I'm supposed to react to that line?" he said. "Look at his hands. Those are field hands? They've never worked a day in his life." When the Hollywood big shots roared, my dad won the part and shortly after became Singin' Sandy.

Once he begged out of this "embarrassing" role, my father said he shattered the mold forever, evolving the Hollywood cowboy into a steely, masculine loner. Still, effeminate cowboys and Singin' Sandy were images he preferred to undo. He couldn't—not completely—and, as a result, I could often hear him reasserting his male persona, even when he bragged about his customized car. *"This* Pontiac station wagon, with *this* special engine, is the best performance car *made."* He once told Peter Bogdanovich, when Mr. Bogdanovich still wrote about film, that a hero in a movie should never cry in the presence of his wife or child. He never said so, but I think my father also meant real life. I can't speak for him and my mother, but he never cried in front of me until their marriage was crumbling, his health was slipping away, and my father knew there was no time left for striking poses.

6

Cutie-pie AISSA WAYNE, 3-year-old daughter of producer-director-star JOHN WAYNE, was the company mascot and general favorite. The little miss also played a part in the picture—one of the children of Mrs. Dickenson whose lives were spared in the massacre at "The Alamo."

—Photo caption in *The Houston Press,*
Jan. 11, 1960

Hung on the wall at my home in Newport Beach, I still have a favorite photograph from the film set of *The Alamo.* Cactus and tumbleweed dotted behind us, we lounge on a shaded porch at the front of a sun-bleached cottage in Texas. As my real dark-haired mother curls my ringlets, I glance at my "mother" in the movie, the beautifully blond Joan O'Brien. His jawline firm, wide shoulders filling a buckskin jacket, my father stands gazing at the prairie. No one faces the camera, no one appearing to know it is there, and we all seem to savor this tranquil Western moment.

Although I was not a child actress, and never had any training, my father cast me in a small part in *The Alamo.* As the movie's producer and director, he told reporters he'd first looked at several child actresses. Then, as I played one morning on our living room rug, my father said he was watching, and my focus on my doll was so intensely undivided, "I knew I'd found my little Dickenson girl." More to the point, I believe, my father had something in common with Francis Ford Coppola: he liked being surrounded and supported by his loved ones when he made movies. There were big rewards and steep falls from glory at stake, and even Hollywood royalty have their self-doubts.

I played Angelina Dickenson, one of the sole survivors of the real Alamo, and some of my earliest memories come from that set. I was not yet four years old, so what I recall is mostly just snippets. My father giving interviews dressed as Davy Crockett . . . a man zestfully playing accordion between takes, as the actor Chill Wills put my feet on top of his own, dancing me and spinning me around, while the cast and crew clapped time . . . pretending I was alseep in my father's leather director's chair so Ken Curtis, the handsome young actor who played my father in the movie, would lift me up and carry me inside to my real parents' trailer.

Not all of my recollections are so idyllic. Most precisely, I recall a moment of abject terror. Before one of my scenes— it would later be cut—I was picked up and put on the back of a cart. The script called for me to hide from the invading Mexican army. Just before my father covered me up with a tarp, he reminded me gently. "This isn't real, Aissa, remember that. It's only a movie. Men dressed as soldiers, holding guns, are going to pull up the tarp. But it's just a movie."

I understood him. When he blocked the sun with the tarp and pitched me into darkness, I didn't lose my composure. I was a paid professional now, earning $250 a week, which my father promised to deposit in my own personal savings account. I knew everyone would be watching me, and I was enjoying the prospect of all their applause and attention. I heard the word *action* and then they yanked the tarp off. The soldiers held bayonets. Unless I hadn't been listening, no one had mentioned these *knife* things at the tip of the rifles. No one had said they'd be tilted at my throat. My scream was real and piercing and shrill.

All I recall after that was being mad at my mother, the cast and crew and stunt men—everyone but my dad. Three and a half years old, I was already learning the pattern.

As I grew up, I came to understand that Hollywood is a labyrinth, a war of attrition, and actually getting movies made and up on the screen is a miracle of finance, persistence, and luck. This, I later learned, was the zigzagging saga of my father's *Alamo.* Getting *The Alamo* researched, thought out, scripted, financed, in front of the cameras, into the can, distributed, and onto the screen took nearly ten years of my father's precious life.

Through the course of the 1950s, my dad was possessed by events that occurred a century before. In 1836, 150 Texans desperately resisted 4,000 Mexican soldiers by defending the Alamo, a San Antonio fortress. By the end of the siege, all the Texans lay dead, and during the rest of their war for independence, Texans cried "Remember the Alamo." An aficionado of American history, my father never saw *The Alamo* as just another action movie. He envisioned it as an epic, with acutely American themes: duty, sacrifice, bravery.

"I hope that seeing the Battle of the Alamo will remind Americans that liberty and freedom don't come cheap," my father told the press. "I hope our children will get a sense of our glorious past, and appreciate the struggle our ancestors made for the precious freedoms we now enjoy—and sometimes just kind of take for granted."

Staunchly patriotic, a political denizen of deep right field, I think my father believed that. But I also suspect he was eager to make *The Alamo* because of a longtime private regret. Although he never discussed it with me, my father himself had never gone to war. Only seven years old when World War I broke out, by December 1941, when the Japanese bombed Pearl Harbor, my father was thirty-four and a father of four. His draft-exempt status notwithstanding, he wanted to serve, but was then under contract to Richard Yates, the ruthless head of Republic Pictures. Not yet a major box office star, still under the autocratic rule of men such as Richard Yates, my father was flatly rebuked. "You should have thought about all that before you signed a new contract," Yates told my father. "If you don't live up to it, I'll sue you for every penny you've got. I'll sue you for every penny you hope to make in the future."

With four children at home, and a lifelong anxiety about money, my dad never went to war. To a man who believed that life largely meant testing one's self, this was an ultimate test untaken. As a result, I think making *The Alamo* became my father's own form of combat. More than an obsession, it was the most intensely personal project of his career.

Beginning at the dawning of the '50s, he pitched it all over Hollywood. He cajoled, argued, seduced and called in old markers. Needing financial backing, and the distribution of a major studio, he flirted with all the top financiers, but each spurned him when he said he had no plans to star in the movie. Instead, he insisted on producing and directing (and having final cut). I think this was partly ego and partly wariness: he did not want his dream distorted by others.

But Hollywood squalked. My father was almost fifty, he'd never directed, and with its size and sweep, this would be a complex and costly project. The studio heads told him to attach a famous director, at minimum, and then come back and see them. Refusing to compromise, my dad took until 1959 to convince a major studio to make the movie on his terms. But United Artists had stipulations of its own. My father had to sign a three-picture deal. He had to star in *The Alamo* as well as produce and direct. His production company, Batjac, had to contribute hefty financing of its own.

That was a problem. Unaware his budget would later double and triple, my father *had* believed at first he could provide most of the finance himself if he had to. After making movies for more than twenty-nine years, he felt sure he had the savings. But my father was never a savvy businessman, nor a careful one. In his John Wayne biography, *Shoot-*

ing Star, Maurice Zolotow wrote: "He was a sucker for a hard luck story. He was a soft touch." It was true. Like his own father, my dad was trusting to a fault. Time after time in his life, he was bilked and exploited. Still, I never quite knew if he was telling the truth when he pleaded poverty, or if we were really in trouble. Because even at the peak of my father's fame, he had a habit of saying we were near-broke. "I have to go to work," he forever insisted. "If I don't make this movie we're all gonna be hurting." Then he'd buy a boat, or a $5,000 dress for my mother, or a Porsche for me the Christmas I turned sixteen. For many years these messages were confusing, until one day I understood: it's true, financially my father is no Bob Hope or Gene Autry. But the man has money. More than anything else, even his restless nature, it's his self-esteem that keeps him working—it is intricately tied up in my father's remaining a star. Once I came to see this about him, his constant working rarely bothered me. Sometimes, at least in this respect, I felt I understood him even better than my mom did.

In 1960, my father's financial problems were shockingly real. When he tried financing *The Alamo* himself, he was told by his personal manager that several of his investments had gone drastically wrong. Rumors flew through Hollywood, and made it into print, that the man had mismanaged millions of my father's dollars. "I had a business manager," my father later told the *Saturday Evening Post,* "who did not do anything illegal, but we were involved in many unfortunate money-losing deals."

Whatever the economic outcome, my dad would have to sort it out later, for he now had a film to get made. To close the deal with United Artists, he scraped up whatever cash he had and promised he could find more if it came to that. Starring my father as Colonel David Crockett, Richard Widmark as Colonel Jim Bowie, and also featuring Laurence Harvey, Richard Boone, Chill Wills, and my half-brother, Patrick Wayne, *The Alamo* was somehow finally born.

Its initial budget was about $7.5 million, remarkably high for those times. Determined to make a film that would endure, my father spared no expense for precise authenticity. To recreate the original fortress town, he commissioned the building of a replica, and this alone exceeded $1 million. He hired 5,000 cast members to ensure that war scenes would look like actual battles, not the same 100 men shot at fifty different angles. Temporary housing had to be constructed. And as I recall, stars and extras alike got to dine on thick Texas steak and lean roast beef. The morale on the *Alamo* set was soaring.

Unfortunately, so was the budget. With such a costly pre-production, before my father ever said "Roll 'em," the United Artists money was gone. With Hollywood grumbling, his dream spinning crazily away, he took radical action. First he wooed a consortium of Texas investors, including Clint Murchison (the wheeler-dealer who'd soon own the Dallas Cowboys). Then he mortgaged our house. He mortgaged Batjac. He mortgaged the family cars, *anything* with capital value—as collateral for loans. "I have everything I own in this picture," he announced, "except my necktie."

Shooting commenced, and continued for eighty-one days. By the end, my producing-directing-starring father had stressed himself to capacity. He weighed thirty pounds less than the day he arrived in the Texas desert. He chain-smoked 100 Camels a day, up from his customary sixty. His smoker's hack never sounded uglier.

All that, and when the movie came out it was mostly panned. A handful of critics praised the acting and realism of *The Alamo* and my father's assured direction of the crucial battle scene. But more ripped its sentimental dialogue and its scene-by-scene flag waving. As for my father, as I will talk about later, he secretly cared much more about the critics than he publicly let on, but he was also never the type of man to sit back and let critics determine his fate. As a response to the bad reviews, and in an effort to recoup his investment, my father launched an aggressively expensive public relations campaign. First, an unprecedented 183-page press release was circulated through Hollywood. Then the town woke morning after morning to full-page trade-paper ads, with bold black headlines like: IT'S UP TO OSCAR. Across Sunset Boulevard, the street where my father officed Batjac and where Hollywood took its lunches, ran this large banner: THIS IS THE MOST IMPORTANT MOTION PICTURE EVER MADE. IT'S TIMELESS. IT WILL RUN FOREVER.

That was not my dad's quote, but by agreeing to use it he came under heavy attack for the ad campaign itself. Although I can see now that his campaign was in fact excessive and grandiose, I think it should be said he was hardly alone. As Hedda Hopper remarked at the time, "What's all this fuss over John Wayne's Oscar ads? People have been buying Oscars for at least twenty-five years." My dad wanted the American public, "the people who go to the movies," as he used to call them, to be the movie's final arbiter. Oscar nominations could make that possible.

This time, he got what he wanted. In spite of another press skirmish over the movie's PR, *The Alamo* received six nominations: best sound, best song, best cinematography, best score, best supporting actor for Chill Wills, and the prize jewel, best movie. Overworked and exhausted, my father felt vindicated and plainly delighted.

Until he saw the ads for Chill Wills.

After his nomination, the man who had danced me around on his feet stomped on my father's hopes for Oscar night. An actor for twenty-five years, apparently Wills saw this as his first and probably last chance for an Oscar. In one of the more outrageous ads Wills placed on his behalf, he listed hundreds of Academy voters by name. "Win, lose, or draw," said the ad, "you're all my cousins and I love you all." With his fine eye for the absurd, Groucho Marx replied with an ad of his own: "Dear Chill, I am delighted to be your cousin, but I voted for Sal Mineo." In another of Chill Wills's ads, the copy read: "We of the *Alamo* cast are praying— harder than the real Texans prayed for their lives in the real Alamo—for Chill Wills to win the Oscar. Cousin Chill's acting was great." Infuriated, my dad quickly tried damage control, running his own ads in *Variety* and *The Hollywood Reporter,* admitting the entire campaign had taken a wild turn, but also making it clear he had not been party to the Chill Wills ads. Signed by my father, the copy read in part, "I refrain from using stronger language because I am sure his (Wills's) intentions were not as bad as his taste."

My mother has told me my father was not surprised on Oscar night when *The Alamo* won only best sound. He was cheered when the film opened well, and so was United Artists, which eventually made a tremendous profit from *The Alamo*'s worldwide release. By then, however, my father could not cash in. To pay off his *Alamo* debts, he'd sold his share of the movie back to UA. While this again made him solvent, he never earned a cent on *The Alamo,* and probably lost a bundle.

Thirty years after he made it, *The Alamo* can still be seen on television; in Texas, a girlfriend told me, they run it at least once every year. Within the Wayne family, we've never considered *The Alamo* a failure. We spoke about it so much during my childhood, I grew up believing it was the finest picture ever made. Although my father toiled on it on and off for ten years, and it drove him to the financial brink, I never heard him complain about how things turned out. True, he was more apt to share with his family his feelings of success than those of disappointment. But given that, I think my father was always a dreamer. I believe it's one of the reasons he loved making Westerns, where he could get out under the stars and be boyish again, riding horses and shooting guns and playing cowboy. For all the heartache and lost money it must have caused him, I think my father understood that he'd given his *Alamo* dream his very best shot, and that this in itself made him a winner.

7

Outside our rented limousine, the swank streets of Manhattan twitched with a palpable energy. With Christmas near, I could see the clouds of breath preceding scurrying shoppers. My first trip to New York, I had many questions about this cold buzzing city as we started and stopped our way through its cluttered traffic. But our heated limousine felt oddly like a museum—silent, stuffy, stagnant, nonconducive to conversation. Though sitting inches away, my father seemed unavailable to me, walled-off by somber thoughts. Peering out the frosted window at the looming thicket of skyscrapers, he barely smoked and spoke not at all. He did not come back outside himself until the chauffeur opened our door and a freezing wind cut holes in our faces.

"Bundle up, honey," he said. "This isn't like winter in California."

Despite his warning, out on the sidewalk my father seemed impervious to the weather. So did the New Yorkers who spotted us, then crowded around us before a doorman could usher us into the building. Though they didn't gush over him overtly, even these hard-to-impress New Yorkers did not appear let down when they saw John Wayne in the flesh. In the cosmetic realm of motion pictures, where actors when glimpsed in person nearly always look smaller and less commanding, my dad was the real thing. Whatever his short-comings, he did not need Hollywood tricks to invest him with size or authority.

As usual, he disarmed the crowd with geniality. Most times this was no act. My dad had faith in ordinary people, and was justifiably singled out by the press for his courtesy, respect, and lack of rudeness with fans. Lately, however, I'd become aware of a metamorphosis—from moody, distracted Daddy to smiling, gregarious star—and I sensed that he was performing. Beneath his cheerful patina, something was distressing my father. Not quite five years old, I just did not know what.

It was late 1960. We were in Manhattan for two reasons: my father had financial business here, and the editors of *Cosmopolitan* had requested our appearance in their magazine. As most Hollywood children did, I would soon begin detesting these publicity sessions, but my memory of this one is pleasing. It was all so spectacular.

Upon our arrival at the photographer's studio, several young angular women fussed over my dad while an older lady, even thinner and prettier, led me to a private dressing room. I was surprised at seeing a man back there, particularly a man in an unattractive blue uniform, wearing a big black gun on his hip, hunched over jewels so bright they positively glistened. Were those for me?

They were! While I held my head regal and still, the pretty lady helped me on with a diamond necklace, diamond bracelet, diamond earrings, diamond broach, and a diamond tiara for my honey-colored hair. I could not believe my own reflection, and was eager to show off for my dad. When I resurfaced for the shooting, he looked as if his breath had been knocked out. He was thunderstruck, I suppose, by this new view of his little girl.

Late that February the magazine hit the newsstands. My, how times and magazines change. It was not until 1965 that Helen Gurley Brown took over *Cosmo* and turned it upside down; now, its cover had nary a blurb about affairs with married men or the latest sexual trends. No sultry, pneumatic Cosmo Girl, as captured by Scavullo, graced the cover photography. Instead, on the the March 1961 issue of *Cosmopolitan,* the cover lines read: Winston Churchill. Hemingway. J. D. Salinger. Pearl S. Buck. Peeking out from beneath those intoxicating names was my smiling face. "John Wayne's daughter, Aissa, wearing $850,000 in Cartier diamonds," read the caption. When my mother showed it to me, it was my turn to feel breathless.

Liking it too, my dad framed the cover and displayed it on his trophy room wall, where one day he'd place his coveted Oscar. He kept stopping at my cover, but he wasn't looking at the jewels. "Your smile is brighter than any diamond, Aissa," my father said. Now I have the cover on my wall, and I must admit the smile I wore that long ago day was appealing. Despite all my glamorous accessories, I wore the sweetly ingenuous smile of a child who believes her unblemished world will never change.

When 1961 rolled in, my father starred in *The Comancheros* for Twentieth Century Fox. Though its cast was substantial—my father, Lee Marvin, Stuart Whitman, the young Ina Belin—the film was memorable only for what it portended. *The Comancheros* marked the first time in my father's career that the script didn't feature a love interest for his character. He was turning fifty-five; it was Stuart Whitman, twenty years younger, who romanced Ina Balin. This foreshadowed the toning down of my father's sexual image on-screen, and led to a critical shift in his life and career.

By the time *The Comancheros* was released, several Hollywood titans had recently passed away. Humphrey Bogart died in 1957, followed by Tyrone Power (1958), Errol Flynn (1959), Clark Gable (1960), and Gary Cooper (1961). Jimmy Cagney had already retired, and Cary Grant would quit in 1962. Of the celestial male stars who launched their careers in the '30s and found stardom in the '40s, only three were making movies at the close of the '60s: Henry Fonda, Jimmy Stewart, and my father.

In his own fifties and sixties, ages at which most leading men have either quit or been not-so-gently phased into minor roles, my father's impact mushroomed. Except for well-paying cameos, he was still the star of all his movies. He still played archetypal American heroes: stubbornly self-reliant, fiercely individualistic, laconic-until-riled loners. But my father portrayed them less and less as romantic leads. Instead he played widowers, brothers, fathers, and grandfathers. He played patriarchal leaders of green but promising soldiers and cowboys. During this cinematic transformation, off-screen my dad waged losing fights with protruding paunch and thinning hair; his face turned craggy and lined; his nose grew more bulbous; and as often befalls heavy smokers, his piercing blue eyes became more lidded by excess skin.

And most Americans only revered him more. In a world going slick and sensationalistic, my father offered them something as priceless as it was powerful—reassurance. As my father aged, he came to stand for maturity, commitment, normalcy, substance, and the way things used to be. For millions of Americans, as Vincent Canby of *The New York Times* wrote, John Wayne became "The almost perfect father figure."

His family saw him in a different light. My father was real to me, not a symbol, and I still have the psychic bruises to prove he was not a perfect father.

And yet when I was still five years old, I too looked at my father with stars in my eyes. With the certainty of innocence, I believed what we had between us would never change. My father would never bully me, and I would never feel hateful.

We would never lie to each other, never feel disappointment in one another, never punish the other with acts of evasion or meanness. As father and daughter, we would never sample the sweets and sours of love. Our love would only be sweet.

It was a lovely myth but it couldn't endure. Unlike my father's movies, no one scripts real life, or real families, and little about them can be predicted. And so, one day on the Hollywood set of *The Comancheros,* my life with my dad began undergoing drastic change.

Another child might have more readily shrugged it off. But until that indelible morning, my father had never shouted at me. He'd never shaken me. The one time he'd nearly spanked me, he was not able to go through with it. I'd spoken disrespectfully back to my mother, my father had unexpectedly entered the room, and he told me to sit outside and contemplate my spanking, because he would be back in two minutes. Sitting on the edge of our cushioned patio chair, I was curiously uncowed. I'd been slapped a few times by my mother, spanked by Angela, our Peruvian maid, and yet I did not believe for an instant my father would hit me—not his little princess. It wasn't until he stepped back outside gripping a leather belt that my eyes filled with tears. When he turned me over his lap, my father raised his belt . . . but I was met with only silence. He suddenly helped me back to my feet, and I saw that my father was settling for a lecture.

Because of our past, I was unprepared for what came that day on the set of *The Comancheros.* Fittingly, for a child of Hollywood, it happened in front of strangers.

As he had in *The Alamo,* my dad had cast me again in one of his pictures. In what was not exactly a stretch for either one of us, he played Jake Cutter, a cantankerous but softhearted Texas Ranger, and I portrayed his adoring grandchild. I don't recall my lines—the scene ended up cut—but I was supposed to deliver them only after I'd fingered my father's neckerchief. As he held me in his arms on his front porch, I ruined the take, forgetting about his neckerchief. Veins in his neck bulging like cords, my father gripped me, and shook me by my shoulders. "You're supposed to play with my tie!" he screamed. "You're supposed to play with my tie!"

My father stared straight at me, but did not seem to be seeing me. Always so focused, his glazed eyes made me frightened, and I felt my body stiffen inside his tensed hands. The kleig lights burned hot as acid churned in my stomach. I could feel the gazes of strangers, cast and crew I barely knew, and I felt deeply self-conscious. I didn't cry, my father released his grip, and somehow I finished the scene correctly. But my father's apologies couldn't slow down my system, or soothe my humiliation. The rest of that day when he came around, telling small jokes and lifting me in the air, I was furtive. Trying to smile and look normal, I did not understand what had happened. But intuitively I knew it meant trouble.

In 1961 my father's life was also changing, in intractable ways I was far too young to understand. It was not just the financial stress from *The Alamo.* In the course of two jarring and melancholic years, several of his oldest friends had died.

Grant Withers, a journeyman character actor, went first at the age of fifty-five. They'd been friends for thirty years, since the days when they'd broken in at Fox, then partied together on John Ford's yacht, the *Araner.* Part of Ford's band of colorful character actors, Grant Withers could always find work but could rarely restrain his behavior off-screen. Including one to Loretta Young, he had five failed marriages, largely due to his drinking. After many attempts at reform and rehabilitation—some of them aided by loans from John Ford and my father—Grant Withers ingested a bottle of tranquilizers and a quart of vodka. His suicide note asked his friends to, "forgive me for letting you down. It's better this way." My mother says my father could not stop shaking when he read these words.

When Ward Bond died next in the winter of 1960, my dad took it much harder. The man I once called "Daddy" was also fifty-five, only two years older than my father, when he suf-

Aissa in her father's embrace (1961)

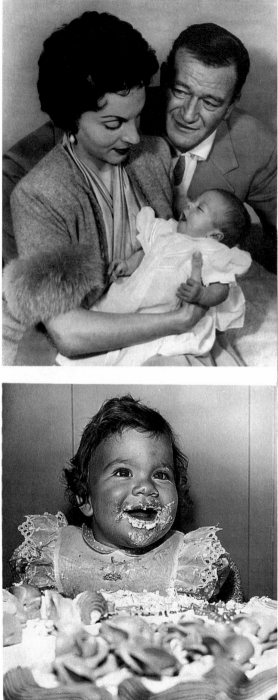

Aissa was a show-biz baby, the true Hollywood princess, fawned over and adored by loving parents (1956).

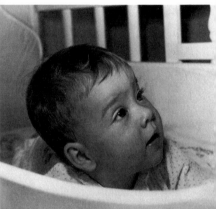

Aissa at six months (1956)

Aissa at one year (1957)

Aissa at age two (1958)

On her second birthday with her father (1958)

Aissa and her mother, Pilar, at home in Encino (1958)

With Pilar and a new bike,
Christmas 1958

John Wayne rose every morning before five-thirty, wired by energy and caffeine—he found satisfaction in a long, hard day's work (1960).

John (clutching a cocktail) with Aissa on the grounds of their five and a half–acre estate in Encino (1951).

John, Aissa, and Pilar in 1959. He loved being surrounded by loved ones.

Aissa's seventh birthday (1963)

Aissa was rarely allowed to play outside with other children out of fear of kidnapping. Her birthday parties were the exception to this rule (1963).

Flocks of multicolored balloons, merry-go-rounds, airplane rides, and live animals were birthday highlights (1963).

John Wayne staged this photo of Aissa (with cigarette)
and Pilarsita (daughter of the Waynes' housekeeper) playing
chess—John's favorite pastime (1963).

As a child, Aissa felt a constant need to be near her father (1963).

"John Wayne's daughter, Aissa, and $850,000 in Cartier Diamonds,"
Cosmopolitan, *March 1961. Aissa was four years old.*

John Wayne's maternal grandfather, Robert Emmet Brown.

John Wayne's maternal grandmother, Margaret Brown.

John Wayne attended USC on a football scholarship.
After injuring his shoulder, he left college at age twenty (1925).

He went on to become
box office gold (1949).

The Sands of Iwo Jima, *1949*.

Rio Grande, *1950*.

The Green Berets, *1967*.

John Wayne with his first wife, Josephine Saenz;
they married in 1933.

Their four children—from left to right—Toni,
Patrick, Melinda, and Michael (1951).

John with wife number two, Esperanza Bauer (Chata) in 1951.

John married Pilar Palette (Aissa's mother) in 1954 in Hawaii.

*John and Pilar. She was
a petite 5'3", 100 lbs., while
he was a burly 6'4", 230 lbs (1955).*

*Aissa and brother Ethan.
She was six when he was born
and quickly appointed herself
his protector (1963).*

Ethan, Pilar, and Aissa (1963)

John and Marissa, his third child from his marriage with Pilar (1968)

fered a massive heart attack in a Dallas hotel room. His whole life, my father said he had never found a closer friend.

Having met playing football at USC, they didn't become buddies until 1928 when they both worked on John Ford's *Salute.* Ford had asked my father to help him cast the movie with football players he knew at USC. My dad didn't ask Bond, considering him a loudmouth, but Bond showed up anyway as the cast was boarding a train to leave for location. Seeing his former teammate, my father called Bond "too ugly for making movies." Bond replied, "Screw you." Ford ordered them both to shut up and get on the train. From this telling moment sprung a three-way friendship only halted by death. My father was drawn to strong, spirited men, unintimidated by life or by John Wayne.

For thirty years, while Bond and my father called John Ford "Pappy" or "Coach," the three men made movies, drank Irish whiskey, played cutthroat bridge, and cheated for pennies at poker. There was plenty of ragging and needling, and all three men were notorious practical jokers. Ford and my father often ganged up on Bond, whose pronounced rear end became their running foil. Once Ford and my dad had their picture taken while standing on either side of a horse's large rump. Bond soon received the snapshot with his pals' inscription: "Thinking of you."

Ward Bond was a hulking physical man, like my father, but when together they were frequently childish. Around Ward Bond, my dad could find release from the pressures of stardom. According to family legend, one boozy night at John Ford's house Bond and my dad were spending the evening when Bond passed out in the bed assigned to my father. Wanting Bond to wake up so the party could continue, my dad poured vodka on his sleeping friend's chest. Igniting it, he then set Ward Bond's chest on fire.

The three men shared more than youthfully wild times. Their affection ran deep and was powerful. For several weeks after Ward Bond left them, my mom says his two friends' grief was unrelievable. The day of his funeral, Bond's body was placed in a flag-draped casket; my father, his resonant voice cracking, spoke the eulogy: "We were the closest of friends, from school days right on through. This is just the way Ward would have wanted it—to look out on the faces of good friends. He was a wonderful, generous, big-hearted man."

By the end of 1961, death was more than a dismal abstract for my father. It had stolen his friends and darkened his world.

With reflection, I know now that the early '60s were a watershed in my father's personal life and in my own life with him. For it was around this time, and increasingly over the next several years as sickness ravaged his patience, that it became harder and harder to salve his insecurities, avoid his temper, and sate his urgent need for his family's attention and love.

It was also the time that I began fearing him. More and more in our home, my father insisted I demonstrate my affection. It might have related to the mortality he must have been feeling. Or perhaps it went all the way back to his relationship with his mother, his sense that she never loved him as much as his younger brother. But I think it mostly had to do with the guilt he suffered after divorcing Josephine, and not being present to raise their four children. "He's still angry at me," my dad warned my mother before she first met Michael Wayne and his other kids with Josephine. "I'm afraid he always will be. It breaks my heart. I let those kids down." He also told my mother, "Don't expect too much from them at first. They haven't forgiven me yet." When my mother said the divorce had been ten years ago, perhaps the children were over it by now, my father just sadly shook his head.

Whatever the cause, he now required ongoing proof of my love. For nearly the next ten years, if he was in a room and I entered it, I could not pass by without kissing him and telling him I loved him. "If you're going through the room, Aissa, come up and give me a kiss," he would say. "You have to kiss me before you can cross by." Our relationship had always been physical, so at first his words seemed harmless. But when it changed from a habit into a rule, I began feeling uneasy, resentful, and threatened. We were not a normal family, remember. We rarely went out to a movie, a dinner, or to Disneyland when we needed some added space from each other, because we knew that people would see John Wayne and we might be mobbed. Now, in supposedly the sanctuary of home life, I felt scrutinized and pressured by my own father. My affection for him, expressed so spontaneously when I was a little girl, sprung from fear and obligation as much as free will. Because if his family failed the test, if my father did not feel smothered in our love, he might erupt. It would never happen right then—he was too prideful and too repressed to admit why he was mad—but several claustrophobic minutes later, and then often triggered by something with scant significance. When my brooding father ignited, his eyes became smaller, harder, darker—almost a steel blue. Since his rage was always delayed and indirect, it all became so unfathomable, so disquieting, trying to decipher what might set him off. So I learned to be cautious of my actions and words. I learned to walk small around my father.

His explosions were not reserved for us. I've been told that he once shoved Richard Widmark up against a wall, on the *Alamo* set, when the actor constantly called into question my father's directing decisions. I only learned of that after he died, but as a child I saw him rage at other people on his film sets. It was awful to witness. Though he never cursed at his family, when my father yelled at adults he peppered his speech with obscenities. I'd cringe and hold my breath until it was over, a tightness inside my throat. I never saw him put his hands on anyone, but he was a powerful man, and I knew he could hurt someone if he chose to. Even today I hate to hear grown men yelling. Even if I know it won't involve me, or can sense it will not end in violence, the yelling makes me jumpy, because sometimes I still hear my father's voice inside their own.

Fortunately, my father's fits of anger had a short life and

no middle ground, extinguishing just as suddenly as they flared. At home, he never sat afterwards and simmered, or transferred the onus to us by claiming we were to blame. His desire to calm me back down, to let me know the mean man inside him had gone, always felt sincere. After every episode, my father immediately, fervently apologized. "Oh my God," he'd always say, "I'm so sorry. I love you, Aissa. I'm so sorry." As I became older and understood more, I could practically see him thinking: *Oh no. I've scared them and now they won't love me. Did they ever?* Then he'd always try winning the love back.

Still, this hardly cured everything. He was not a normal-sized man and his voice was loud to begin with. When his body and voice were charged with hostility, my father shrunk the scale of everything around him. At times I felt so tiny I thought he might shout me into the floor. No matter how earnest, no amount of contrition could undo all that.

No one can say for sure what makes human beings act as they do, what fills them with such ire, but I don't think my father ever *intended* to hurt us or frighten us. I don't think he blew up with premeditation, or took pleasure from the cringing expressions we wore on our faces. It is, I think, a common trait among men whose psyches crash back and forth between pride and insecurity: my father lashed out when he felt himself getting weak.

8

When I was in kindergarten, one of the local television affiliates dubbed Tuesday evenings "John Wayne Night." For the sake of his fans in Los Angeles County, they faithfully aired *Red River,* or *The Searchers,* or *The Wings of Eagles,* or my personal favorite, *The Quiet Man.* Watching cartoons one weekend morning with my mother's girlfriend's daughter, I turned to her and said, "My daddy's on TV every Tuesday night. What night is your daddy on TV?"

If a child's purity provides its own best protection, it's all too brief and fragile. More so, perhaps, if the child is born to a man called Duke, a man on a first-name basis with America. Throughout my abnormal childhood, in layers and by degrees, the special burdens and blessings of inherited fame revealed themselves to me. As the daughter of a Hollywood superstar, I frequently basked in the aura of being called "Wayne." But sometime I wanted out from beneath the weight of my father's gigantic stature, out from inside his shadow, where I could just be myself, whoever that might be.

As John Wayne's child, it was difficult to tell.

Making self-discovery even murkier, my childhood was filled with artifice. When my father and I were under the public stare, or on exhibit for the press, I found myself endlessly posturing. I might be famished or crabby, my parents might have just scolded me in the car, but I had to mask my emotions, smiling angelically for the clamoring paparazzi when invariably they said: "Stop, Duke. Let's take a picture of you and your family." In moderation this was tolerable, even flattering, but paparazzi and moderation do not co-exist. *Pop-pop-pop-pop-pop-pop.* When one is an otherwise-sheltered child, the sound becomes a form of shell shock.

Inside our home, when we opened our doors to notebooks and cameras, my behavior had to be just as carefully modulated. As did most public figures, my father understood the value of the press and also the damage it could unleash. After his messy, highly public divorce to Chata, he had earned a reputation as a hard-drinking womanizer and hell-raiser. As a corrective, he had since worked very hard at rebuilding his all-American, family-man image. It was not all public relations, but there existed a sizeable gap between veneer and reality, between the beaming, nurturing clan we presented to the American public and family life as we actually lived it. Determined to keep this family picture pristine, my father took no chances. In the presence of the inquiring press, he forbade even a trace of domestic upheaval. As an appendage to his image, I was conditioned to wear my best clothes and most luminous smile and pretend that life as a Wayne was always idyllic. As instructed by my dad, I spoke politely only when spoken to, and never became expansive.

"If you don't open your mouth, Aissa, then you can't get in trouble," he told me repeatedly throughout my childhood and, without fail, prior to any meeting with the press. "The only way to get in trouble, the only way for people to think you're a jerk, is if you open your mouth."

If this was fundamentally correct, perhaps it was not the best advice to an overdependent young girl who would one day become a woman and no longer have her father to orchestrate her life. Through my puberty, adolescence, and young womanhood, my father's strongly stated words stayed with me. Still playing Daddy's Little Girl, I tried to look pretty, shrunk from all confrontations, let my father solve my problems, kept my convictions to myself. After my father died and I had no choice but to try and grow up, even then I found it hard to express my opinions. I didn't *know* what I believed in. My Hollywood princess childhood, my controlling father—and my own willingness to be treated this way, long after I should have known better—had not prepared me to think and act for myself.

As a child, I hated most formalized photo sessions. Bad enough that the implicit threat of my father's authority was enough to make me nervous and censor my words. Bad enough that I acted so phony, more like some Hollywood cliché of a little girl—prim, poised, proper, and perfect— than a bonafide flesh-and-blood child. But on top of all that, the process itself numbed the childhood mind. Granted, some talented and considerate media and Hollywood studio photographers moved in and out and let us return to our lives. But others wanted every camera angle, against every backdrop on our estate, as insurance they would not squander their chance to photograph a major star. And instead of relieving the pressure, often my father turned it up.

"Come over here," he'd mutter so only I could hear him. "Closer. Put your arm around me. Smile. Just pretend you love me, okay?"

Since I didn't have to pretend, I felt some resentment at having to prove to the world, to strangers, how much the Wayne family adored one another. Advertising our love seemed to make it less real, to diminish it.

In the way of many children of rich and famous parents, I suppose I wanted it both ways. At times I enjoyed conspiring with my father in keeping his image bright and shining, and at times I felt sickened by all the calculation. I craved for people to love me the way they loved him, and I wanted to be left alone. I clung to my position on the pedestal, using my family name to meet important people, to get into USC without having the grades, and yet fantasized many nights about being a normal child.

The latter wasn't feasible, of course. Normal children did not go to the Academy Awards or meet Frank Sinatra. Their mothers did not come home happily sloshed from lunch because Liz Taylor had insisted on ordering two martinis per person, per round. And normal children did not stand in the wings at industry functions watching Hollywood wannabes and hangers-on literally standing in line, waiting to pay homage to their fathers. When his fans received their turn, they all but knelt at the shrine of John Wayne. They wooed him, flattered him, desperately tried to impress him with their wit. I'd watch my surrounded father at these affairs, pondering if he enjoyed it or if he abhorred it. Although they were all around him, it seemed to me they did not want to know him, but only to try and absorb the special light that shone on John Wayne.

At such strange moments I'd always feel some loneliness myself, some jealousy and deprivation. *Who were these unctuous strangers and why was he paying more attention to them?* Nevertheless, these incidents paled when held next to what happened in Madrid when I was seven years old.

In 1963, my family accompanied my father to Spain for the filming of *Circus World.* With my dad working fourteen-hour days for director Henry Hathaway, I was thrilled when he awoke one day and said his morning was free: How would I like to stroll, only the two of us, through a village on the outskirts of Madrid? On days off like this, when my father felt guilty about working long hours, I often asked him for presents. I tried not to, knowing it was wrong, but I couldn't help myself. My father said yes when I asked him that morning, but the festive-looking storefronts weren't quite open for business. That was fine with me. In between the shops on either side, the red-brick courtyard was dotted by pretty trees and fountains. It was a cloudless immaculate day and no one had noticed my father. How buoyant life felt at that moment.

As if to prove that life never comes as advertised, and that even sunny days can turn horrific, our trouble started then. I saw three men trotting in our direction, smiling and surely friendly, yet I felt my father's hand close tighter around my own. He began moving faster, away from the stores, toward the more spacious middle of the courtyard, and now the people were screaming: "HEY JOHN WAYNE! HEY JOHN WAYNE! DUKE—DUKE!" Quickly there were more than three men. There were several, then dozens, then so many I couldn't count them. The throng was mostly men, yet even some women and children seemed angry. I didn't understand. Spain was so beatific, and the Spanish so loved my dad. They especially flocked to his Westerns and for years took pride when the Spanish press reported that all three Mrs. John Waynes had been Latins.

Then the crush of human bodies came upon us. A man ripped at my father's shirt and the rest of the pack grew braver. Hands clawed at my father's pants, his hair, his neck, and then people were *jabbing, jabbing, jabbing,* pointed pens and autograph books, inches from my father's crimson face. Still clutching my left hand, he was shoved ahead of me—I felt a yanking pain in the socket of my left shoulder.

"Get off, get off!" my father screamed. "Get the fuck *off!*" With one hand he reeled me back to him; with the other he reached for the cards in his pocket. Knowing his allure to the Europeans, before we'd left America my father had had cards printed bearing his name and autograph. Before that morning in Madrid, the other times that we'd appeared in public, his cards had appeased the crowds of fans who gathered to see America's John Wayne. In fact, he had grown so dependent on his cards, he'd become paranoid the few times he'd forgotten them.

This time the cards could not help us. I saw no reverence in this morning's faces; some faces looked contorted in fury. A skinny man with bugging eyes tried swiping the stack of cards from my father's hand and a bigger man threw a looping punch at the first. My dad flung the cards high in the air and behind him, and some people broke off to fight for the cards. Through the churning feet and legs, I saw an old man bend down to snatch a card and be kicked in the face by a boy. The back of my legs gone numb, I was struck in the small of my back by what felt like a pointed knee and my breath rushed out as my hand was torn from my father's. Shoved and turned and smothered, now I was on the ground screaming: "DADDY! DADDY! DADDY!"

I couldn't see him. "DADDY!"

"AISSA? AISSA? GODDD-DAMMMIT!"

I heard my father's voice, stood up, tried to locate it. Thank God he was tall—as the mob surged back toward the storefronts, I saw only the top of his head poking out above the swarm. The sight of him, surrounded, flooded my system with so much adrenaline my body started trembling, and I felt my terror mixing with hatred. Running and thrashing to get myself back to my dad, I overran the pack, then flung myself back into it. Still screaming "DADDY," I felt sickened by the stink of perspiration. Somehow my father did the rest. Barking "Aissa!" he grabbed my wrist as a door flew open. We stumbled inside and a small mustachioed man slammed the door behind us, hurried and locked it. Seeing it myself made it no more believable: people pressed their faces into the shopkeeper's glass. They banged with fists and scratched with fingernails. The three of us stared at the humans gone haywire, then the shopkeeper yelled, *"Policia, policia,"* and my father pulled me away toward the back of the store. Still wheezing and red faced, still screaming "bastards," my father appeared unharmed, having lost nothing more than his poise. Turning me around so my back faced the mob, he said, "It's over, honey, it's over now." But I couldn't stop crying and stuttering. Waiting for the police, I asked no questions, and my father had no explanations. I wished we had never set foot in Spain. I wished that my father was not so monstrously famous.

9

I don't recall when I first became mischievous. But I know it happened early, and that I was intensely circumspect around my dad. Still, this did not deter me from misbehaving when he was not around. As an acolyte to a carefully scrutinized Hollywood emperor, my chances to be naughty were too temptingly rare. During my adolescence in Newport Beach in the early '70s, my rebellions would grow bolder with the recklessness of the times. Unknown to the press or my dad, I experimented with diet pills, marijuana, and getting arrested. As a child in Encino, I settled for terrorizing our maids.

Aside from my father's exalted celebrity, his financial need and mental compulsion to work hard and often, he and my mother back then were still very social creatures. There were charity events, dinner parties, movie openings, Republican fundraisers. To attend to the housework and aid with my supervision, my mother hired two Peruvian maids. Consuela and Angela Saldana were dark-haired sisters, brought from Latin America to Southern California while both were in their twenties. They were part of the fabric of my childhood, and I did horrible things to each of them.

Consuela was younger and more credulous; for the first few years I could always fool her. I performed evil acts when she wasn't looking, then, when confronted, I resumed being the Good Aissa, and sweetly naïve Consuela believed my paper-thin lies. Even after I began tormenting her openly, Consuela did not have it in her to inform on me to my parents. One evening my parents entertained friends for late dinner, and I disobeyed Consuela when she told me it was bedtime. Feeling I had a better idea, I ran from my upstairs bedroom into my parents', jumping up and down on their enormous bed. Consuela followed, leaning toward me and gently explaining why a young girl needed her rest. I stopped leaping and startled both of us, reaching out and grabbing Consuela's midnight-black hair.

"I am not going to bed!" I hissed. Fixated on my own balled fist, I unpried my fingers.

Rubbing her scalp as she moved for the door, Consuela said softly, "This time, I am telling your father."

That wouldn't do.

My father had never seen the other Aissa, the Bad Aissa. Part of me wanted to know: Could he see this unpleasant side of me and still love me? Fearful the answer might be no, I scrambled off my parents' bed and into the hallway.

Watching Consuela wind calmly down our spiral staircase, still maintaining her dignity, prompted me to entirely surrender mine. Inexplicably furious, I leaned over the railing and spit. For a moment Consuela stood still as a picture, then she turned back upstairs with a near imperceptible glance at the saliva on her blue cotton blouse. Avoiding my eyes, she looked not incensed but profoundly unhappy. Considering an excuse, I bolted instead for my room and started whimpering. How cruel she was for making me do what I did.

Consuela never snitched. Though from time to time I still abused her, something had altered between us, and I found myself drifting to her older sister. Slightly built and completely self-contained, Angela Saldana never wore lipstick or makeup. Her one arresting feature—her scuplted cheekbones—were made to look severe by her paper-fine cropped-off black hair. Having hired Angela first, and then Consuela in the wake of her older sister's excellence, my parents trusted Angela unconditionally, and gave her permission to treat me as she saw fit. Back in Encino, in some ways it was Angela who raised me. At that point in my life, my parents were still like fairy tale characters to me: grand, beautiful characters whom I loved, but characters living refracted lives, which I had to share with many others. Mornings, it was Angela who dressed me and bathed me. At night, Angela stood guard while I brushed my teeth, then ensured that I flick off my flashlight and stop sneak-reading books under my covers. Unlike Consuela, there was no duping the older sister. From the beginning, Angela Saldana saw right through me. That she knew who I was and still seemed approving made me love her madly.

Still, my affection for our maid earned me no slack. In Angela's sturdy presence every transgression had a consequence. She never spanked me in front of my father, since then I gave her no reason, but when we were alone she spanked me frequently, wholeheartedly, grabbing me on the run as I tried to escape. Acting in place of my parents when they were away, Angela felt it her duty to enforce discipline. In the absence of my parents—and other children to play with—I felt it my duty to drive her insane.

Once I was angry at her for demanding I shed my clothes "this minute" and climb into my bath. First assuring Angela I would, I went instead, fully clothed, to our laundry chute. Its door was built into our second-floor wall, outside the bedrooms. Our dirty clothes dropped down to the first floor, in a pantry bin adjacent to our kitchen. Aware that Angela was down there cleaning, I took knee socks from my drawer and stuffed them with other clothes until they bulged. I jammed the feet end of the socks into a pair of my ballet slippers. Hanging the slippers and fake human legs down the chute, shutting the metal door to wedge them in place, I banged on the door and screamed bloody murder. Then I abruptly stopped. I wanted Angela to spy the dangling legs, think I had fallen in and had ceased yelling because I'd blacked out. And then died.

Perfection. First I heard Angela shouting "AISSA!" Then came her clicking shoes on our staircase. When she burst into my room I sat on the edge of my bed, chuckling. Her dark face swelling with incoming blood, Angela cursed me in Spanish. Already speaking my mother's first language fluently, I recognized some words and caught the jist of the rest. Then Angela took her familiar hand to my bottom.

Having never returned to her native Peru, today Angela still lives in Los Angeles, in a cozy home my father bought for her when my family left the huge Encino estate for a much smaller house in Newport Beach. Thirty-five years after we met, Angela and I still speak on the phone, still deeply missing the man from whom we kept secrets.

10

A fter the deaths of Grant Withers and Ward Bond, John Ford sought comfort in the church, rediscovering the Irish Catholic religion of his childhood. For my less-spiritual father, no such retreat was possible. Though believing in Jesus Christ and God, my father never once went with my mother and me to our Catholic church, and was skeptical as a rule toward organized religion. When asked, he used to refer to himself with a grin as a "Presby-goddamn-terian."

At the beginning of 1962, my father could muster none of his good humor. For such a large man, John Ford once said of him, "John Wayne moves with the grace of a dancer." But during my father's severe depression, a time when life seemed little more than a series of bereavements, he moved slowly, almost ploddingly. He was so filled with sadness for his friends, even immersing himself in work could not dispel the heaviness that came over him. Watching my dad at home, I had never seen him so inactive. He looked, at times, to be struggling to merely get out of his chair.

Thank goodness he liked babies. A man who lived to see twenty-one of his grandchildren, there were few things that lifted his spirits the way one more little Wayne did. And at six in the morning on February 22, 1962, my father found solace in perhaps the only place he really could, from his family, when my mother gave birth to a second child.

My mother bore John Ethan Wayne after agonizing through another protracted labor, this one nearly as long as when she had me. But my brother was born without complications, a godsend in light of my mother's harrowing past. In the six years since she had bore me, my mother had suffered three miscarriages. One, in 1959, was made public by an overeager confidant of my dad who revealed my mother's pregnancy prematurely—to Louella Parsons. That spring, the gossip columnist printed that my parents were expecting. Several days later, my father had to announce that his wife had lost the baby. As part of the price for being Mrs. John Wayne, my mother's intensely private loss became a public event.

In 1961, the doctors confirmed my mom was once again pregnant, but for all their powers could not guarantee she would carry to term. The next several months she alternated between elation and fear. One night, she and I sat alone on my parents' bed and my mother spoke in almost a whisper about "my history," and "past complications." Vaguely aware of her meaning, there was no mistaking the anguish in her eyes.

But this time it was all worth it. Through the miracle of life, a family of three was now four. Six years old when Ethan was born, I recall no feelings of jealousy. Though losing my status as an only child, all I remember is my excitement, that our estate would now contain another small person, and perhaps I would not feel so lonesome. My mother recalls it differently. When Ethan was born, she says my first words upon seeing him in the hospital were, "Look, Mommy, I hurt my finger."

When my little brother came home with his red wriggling body and my father's blue-lagoon eyes, I anointed myself his protector. I rocked him and fed him and hushed his bawling, surprised myself with the mother in me. The second day we had him, my parents allowed me to burp our new baby. Ethan spit up on my shoulder, and all of us started laughing, even my dad. I had not heard that sound in so many weeks I'd feared it had left our lives forever.

Not long after Ethan's birth, my father again fell prone to bouts of depression. Perhaps receiving one new life reminded him of the death of his friends. Slowly, however, Ethan reminded my dad that he needed to keep moving forward. For his entire adulthood, my father had felt a need to provide, to accomplish, to prove himself. Finally, these needs of my father came back, and he dove once again into making pictures.

Still recovering from the cost of *The Alamo* and a few soured investments, what he needed now wasn't meetings or memos or concepts or promises—"Hollywood blah blah blah," as he called it. With a wife, an ex-wife, six children from two different families and a pair of grandkids (Michael's Alicia and Toni's Anita) he needed money, and needed it quickly. First he closed a crucial negotiation with Paramount Pictures. They would pay him $600,000 a movie for ten movies. This was at least $100,000 under his current price, but the contract was nonexclusive, and Paramount agreed to pay much of the $6 million up front. This meant erasing old debts, revitalizing Batjac, feeding mouths, and paying employees—a prospect my father could not resist. Despite a downbeat, much-discussed profile that ran that year in the *Saturday Evening Post*—"The Woes of Box Office King John Wayne"—in truth my dad had embarked on financial resurrection.

Economic help came next from an improbable source—Darryl Zanuck. Only one year before, in 1961, he and my father had publicly collided. A onetime screenwriter, Darryl Zanuck had gotten his break in the 1920s, penning the adventures of a fearless German shepherd. After writing stories for Rin Tin Tin, Zanuck later founded the company that would become Twentieth Century Fox. Firmly entrenched as a Hollywood "mogul," the megalomaniacal, cigar-chomping Zanuck came courting my father in 1962. Six years earlier, he'd resigned his post at Fox and moved to Europe, triggering the once-vaunted studio's slide to the edge of ruin. Returning to Fox as president, Zanuck's plan for saving it hinged around his pet project, *The Longest Day,* the epic depicting the D-Day invasion of France. Normally, my father was anxious to pay tribute on-screen to American soldiers, but when Zanuck inquired he flatly refused to star in *The Longest Day.* He was still too angry for what Zanuck had done to him just two years earlier.

During the pre-Oscar uproar over *The Alamo,* the man called DFZ had stung him. Speaking to a reporter in Paris, but knowing his biting words would reverberate all through Hollywood, Zanuck blasted Kirk Douglas, Burt Lancaster, Marlon Brando, Richard Widmark, and most prominently John Wayne. All were actors who'd formed their own production companies. Like many of Hollywood's old guard, Zanuck felt actors, even famous, bankable actors, should still be treated by the studios as attractive pieces of *merchandise.* When my father starred, directed, and produced *The Alamo,* Zanuck felt it akin to inmates running the asylum.

"I've got a great affection for Duke Wayne," Zanuck was quoted in Paris, "but what right has he to write, direct, and produce a motion picture? Look at poor old Duke now. He's never going to see a nickel, and he put all his money into finishing *The Alamo.*"

Infuriated at the patronizing tone—poor old Duke?—my father fired back. "It's SOB's like Zanuck that made me become a producer. Who the hell does he think he is, asking what right I have to make a picture? What right does he have to make one?" In reality, my father respected him. He said Zanuck truly loved movies, not just profit, and unlike many executives, always had the guts to trust his own hunches. Still, when Zanuck phoned from Europe in 1962 regarding *The Longest Day,* my father coldly said he had no interest. Zanuck, like my dad, unaccustomed to being told no, only doubled his transatlantic hounding, upping his price each phone call. Finally, my father agreed to perform a cameo, and even that with a stipulation: his price tag for those few days was a quarter of a million dollars. Certain he'd driven his price to unmeetable heights, my father was shocked when Zanuck met it. Proudly, but not blindly, my dad jetted to Europe, went before the camera for only four days, and earned nearly ten times more for his cameo than Henry Fonda, Sean Connery, and Richard Burton did for their own.

The prescient Zanuck didn't mind. Boosted by my father's box office pull, and in tandem with Fox's *The Sound of Music, The Longest Day* returned the flailing studio into the black.

"It was highway robbery," my father later admitted privately. "But I needed the money at the time, and that bastard Zanuck had it coming."

11

In 1962, his year of rebirth and renewal, my dad was also recruited by Howard Hawks, the distinguished director of *Bringing Up Baby, Sergeant York,* and *Gentlemen Prefer Blondes.* Hawks asked him to join him in Africa, to star as a big-game hunter in *Hatari!* His faith in Hawks unequivocal, my father said yes without hesitation.

They'd worked together once before, in 1947, when Hawks made *Red River,* starring my dad as Thomas Dunston and Montgomery Clift as his son. Clift's first screen role and Howard Hawks's first Western, *Red River* was a great commercial and artistic success. Playing a myopic sadistic cattle baron who relentlessly drives his men to mutiny, my father showed acting skills much broader than perhaps even he suspected. If John Ford's *Stagecoach* proved John Wayne could carry a major motion picture, Hawks' *Red River* made him a star. What's more, Howard Hawks came to *Red River* a novice to Westerns, unable to discern healthy cattle from those half dead, or true Western actors and stuntmen from big-talking pretenders. Montgomery Clift, straight out of the theatre, said he arrived on the set not knowing how to ride a horse or shoot a gun or walk in cowboy boots. Without condescending, my father coached them both. When the movie came out and kudos poured in for all three talented men, Howard Hawks kept telling the press, "I couldn't have made *Red River* without John Wayne."

It was this gentlemanly quality, and his respect for Hawks's work, that prompted my dad to fly to the distant side of the world in late 1962. When he invited my mother and me to join him, I was delighted. Not giving our destination much further thought, I soon learned what Hollywood meant by "exotic location."

Most of the film was shot on the Serengeti Plain of Tanganyika (Tanzania), at the base of Mount Meru, the gargantuan twin of Kilimanjaro. On my first day on the high plains of the Serengeti, it must have soared past 100 degrees, and I felt so hot I thought I would never be cool again. That night I realized I'd been wrong—with sunset came some relief— but that's also when the plains became extraordinarily noisy. Lying in my bed beneath a suspended mesh net, I was safe from the bloodthirsty bugs, but could not tune out the strange sounds of screaming, yowling, jabbering, honking African beasts. To me, every animal's sound meant another threat.

For the next few days, I felt so tired I told my father no when he asked if I wanted to watch him film out in the wild. The long ride on the plane and the shortness of sleep had worn me down, so I stayed behind with my mother. About the third or fourth afternoon, standing beneath a tree, I heard a screech, then felt something jump on my back. I screamed, flailing at my attacker, and a small monkey stopped clawing at my hair and scurried back up the tree it had dived from. I wasn't hurt or even knocked off my feet, only unnerved, but my wild animal problems were just beginning.

Told by the local residents how to thwart the malicious monkeys—don't stand under trees—I turned one morning to see a much odder creature: It had a long skinny bare neck, black-feathered-medicine-ball of a body, and long skinny bare legs. The ostrich was walking directly toward me, and I took off running. Unbeknownst to me, this was precisely how not to react; once human beings run, ostriches will give chase. Though my back was turned, I could feel the excited animal closing the gap with its massive stride. Then a little African boy, no taller than I, ran shouting right past me, and when I turned back the ostrich had taken flight in the other direction. While I tried to control my shaking I returned the shy smile of the little boy who'd saved me.

Making his movie, meanwhile, my father was having adventures of his own. Doing his own stunt work one day, he hung off the side of a moving Land Rover during a zebra-hunting scene. From the blind side of the jeep rushed an uninvited bull rhinocerous. The startled driver veered, the jeep bucked, almost flipping, and my father was nearly cata-pulted into what might have been a fatal landing. That night when he returned for dinner everyone seemed so caught up in his thrilling tale. So I didn't talk any more about the os-trich or monkeys.

Or the baby elephants. A few days into my visit, my fa-ther had introduced me to three of them; he and Howard Hawks were using them in their movie. The baby elephants really did seem friendly, especially when compared to the ostrich and monkeys. But my father did not take into account that, to me, "baby elephant" was a cruel misnomer. Silently angry and panicked—thinking, *Why are you making me do this?*—I allowed him to stick me on one of their backs while the cameras went *pop-pop-pop-pop.* Time, as it is apt to do during crises, started crawling as the leviathan baby took off. At that interminable moment, I sought nothing more out of life than my return to solid ground, and yet all I did was smile through clenched teeth. Because I could not talk to my father, because he sometimes treated me like an object instead of a child, I rode in fear while he stood grinning and watching.

Later that week, a buzz came over the set from out in the wild. A great male African elephant, typically easygoing, had gotten separated from his herd. Dangerous now, the outcast had charged the men on the film set, including my dad, and he and the men had killed it.

This much made sense to me. I'd seen the men on the sets holding high-caliber rifles, and by then I understood the Serengeti's peril. The men had killed the wild elephant to save their own lives. Much better the elephant than my father, I told myself, as my mother and I motored over the plains to the sight where the men were filming.

When we arrived the pieces stopped fitting. Except for its behemoth size and blood-darkened skin, the slain elephant looked a lot like the babies I'd been riding. All week long, the adults all told me the babies were my friends, so I'd started trying to think of them that way. Now, many of the Americans were taking pictures near the prone animal, and my father told my mother and me to go and stand in front of it. In the scorching African heat, the blood smell was so strong it filled my lungs and nose and I thought I might throw up. Although by standing perfectly still I managed not to gag, I felt so light I thought I might float off the earth. Sad, sick, and confused, I let my mother take me back to the car.

Stateside a few months later I turned seven years old and my parents staged my annual birthday party. Even my father, who deplored most of Hollywood's flashier tribal customs, relented when it came to my parties. Perhaps he knew I was starved for playtime with other children, seeing them so scarcely except at school. Perhaps, like so many stars, he felt trapped between the antagonistic demands of Hollywood and family, and felt he could tip back the scale by throwing me extravagant parties.

I do think my elaborate birthday parties were for my sake, and not for his. Publicity games were one thing; social-status games my father roundly rejected, finding them both ridiculous and degrading. And to both my parents' credit, they never indulged in the hoariest Hollywood practice of all: inviting other movie stars' children, kids I didn't know, in the twisted hope that their famous mommies and daddies would also stop by for cake and ice cream, so my parties might enhance my parents' social reputation. Except for little Dean and Gina Martin, Dean and Jeanne's two children, both of whom I'd always liked, my parents invited only my classmates. I realize it's de rigueur for children of Hollywood to say they loathed their birthday parties, to describe the other industry kids as starched and nervous and grim faced, and to trash their movie star parents for putting them through them. But except for one, I enjoyed my parties immensely. In our backyard we had merry-go-rounds and "airplane" rides, bunches of multicolored balloons, brightly dressed men wielding cotton candy, and pretty ponies for rides across our green expanse of lawn. Had my guests been other star children, it all might have been oddly passé. But the children from my school, unjaded by Hollywood, were so dreamy-eyed at my parties it always infected me.

The one party I didn't like was this one when I turned seven following our trip to Africa. That spring morning, my mother told me to play in my room while she and my father put the finishing touches on our yard. Play? I was far too concerned with my appearance. My taste on such occasions ran to white. Though the party would not start for a couple of hours, I already had on my winter white organdy dress, my glittering white shoes and socks, and my white satin ribbons bedecking my dainty curls. Not long after she told me to go in and play, my mother interrupted my preening.

"Your father has a question about the party," she said. "Can you come outside?"

Who did she think she was kidding? For one thing, my parents planned my parties with painstaking precision. Except for making out my guest list and vetoing clowns—I thought they looked sinister—my input had never been solicited. For another thing, both she and I knew that my father was always full of surprises. It was one of his special charms. Once, on a lengthy, potentially endless-seeming plane ride from Los Angeles to Europe, he purchased the entire first class for him and my mother, making it unforgettably romantic. On the morning of one of my earliest birthdays, he'd come into my room and drawn my bedroom drapes, revealing a life-size playhouse in our backyard. While I'd slept during the night, my father had snuck in the workers to construct it.

Prepared to be surprised by my special gift, I was flabbergasted anyway. Outside in front of our pool, three feet from my dad, stood one of my African "friends."

A baby elephant.

As if still on Howard Hawks's cue, it stuck its trunk in the pool and sprayed water all over the deck and my dad.

When I first saw the gray animal I was speechless, overcome by all these *feelings.* First, I was astounded. Then I felt queasy, the movie screen of my mind flashing back on the wild elephant, lying rotting and dead among the flies and the stench that horrible day in the African plains. Then I considered the baby elephant and my father. As he had so many times back there, he'd make me ride the elephant today, in front of all the children from my school. I'd smile prettily for all and my dad would still not see I was frightened. This last thought disheartened me: my own father could not tell my counterfeit smiles from my real ones.

My mother cleared her throat, my signal to speak. I focused again on my dad, standing in front of our pool in the white morning sunlight. Where the baby elephant doused him, his formerly clean pressed clothes were wet and mildly rumpled. He wasn't scowling or fuming or raising his voice, though. He was smiling at me and although his tears never spilled I could see his eyes welling with happiness. He had no idea what was going through my head.

But it didn't mean he didn't love me; that he loved me was never in doubt. Without feeling I had to, I ran and squeezed him and let him hold me as long as he wanted.

Returning inside, though, I promised myself I would not

ride the baby elephant. Not in front of my classmates, not on my birthday, no matter how much trouble he must have gone to. For just this one day, I would not sublimate myself, while he treated me like a possession. I would not do whatever my father wanted me to, and pretend it made me sublimely happy.

That afternoon I rode the baby elephant.

12

I n 1963 I missed second grade entirely when my father decided to take his dream trip, on his dream ship, in what looked at first like our dream family vacation.

Around the time Ethan was born my father had purchased *The Wild Goose* with the money he earned from Paramount. It was not his first boat, but the first befitting my father's own bigness. *The Wild Goose* was 136 feet of converted World War II minesweeper, with the finest engines and navigational equipment. Once my father remodeled, her accomodations included an oak-paneled master salon with a wet bar, a wood-burning fireplace, a motion picture projector and screen, and a teleprinter receiving UPI, AP, and weather bureau reports; a luxurious master suite and three guest staterooms, each with its own bath; a dining room that comfortably sat ten; a sixty-foot afterdeck for sunning and playing cards; a cast-iron barbecue; a washer-dryer; a liquor locker; and a wine cellar.

When my father wasn't working, *The Wild Goose* had a strong psychic pull for him. In the winter, we took it to Acapulco; most summers we cruised to Alaska. For my father and other famous leading men, yachting was a venerable tradition. In many ways enslaved by their outlandish celebrity, stars like Humphrey Bogart, Jimmy Cagney, and Errol Flynn all found asylum on the sea. By the summer of 1963, my father had launched a love affair with *The Wild Goose* that would continue unabated until his final years. By then we'd already taken *The Goose* from Newport Beach to the Baja coast, but these trips had been leisurely. To challenge his brawny new ship, my father was eager to find a stiffer test. When Henry Hathaway asked him to star with Rita Hayworth in *Circus World,* a film he planned shooting in Spain, my father found his crucible. He told Hathaway yes, he would be in Madrid that September, delivered there by *The Wild Goose.*

As my father breathlessly explained it, leaning over the maps spread on the desk in his trophy room, we would start down for Acapulco, then steam around the Mexican coast and on through the Panama Canal. From there we'd traverse the Gulf of Mexico and dock in Bermuda, where Ethan, my mother, and I would disembark. Feeling this leg of the trip too jeopardous for his wife and young children, he and a crew of eight would strike out alone across the Atlantic. We'd rejoin them on the Portuguese coast, lingering at several ports up to and beyond the tip of Spain.

When the notion took hold of me, I was giddy with the prospect of flight and adventure. An entire year away from our compound, much of it in Spain, and no school except for a tutor! Spain sounded gay and sunny, and having a Latin mother and two Latin maids, I already spoke Spanish. I also sensed that my father needed this badly. In the final weeks before we set off, he'd started behaving erratically. One moment he'd be animated and loquacious, detailing the newest wrinkle in our itinerary or his latest renovation to *The Goose,* and the next moment he'd be somber and mute. On the queerest night of all, my father had entered my bedroom and pulled me to his chest without speaking.

"Aissa?" he'd finally said, a stiffness to his voice that told me something wasn't right.

"Yes, Daddy?

"When you get older and you realize I'm not as strong as you think I am, will you still love me?"

"Yes, Daddy."

Always with my father it was "Yes, Daddy," and I said it that moment by rote. In truth I was disconcerted. Why was he acting so unlike himself, the dynamic self I relied on so utterly—even more, it sometimes seemed, than water and air?

I knew he was hurting inside. Every day his smoker's hack sounded uglier and more raw. And I'd seen the wadded tissues littering his side of their bed, the tissues at times streaked reddish-yellow, what I knew was his blood mixed with phlegm. At some subconscious level, I understood these things threatened me, but I didn't add them together, and so did not yet know the sum of my fears. Hating when things were obscure to me, I felt increasingly eager to launch our trip.

And then we were off! From the day we left the dock at Newport my father was never easier to be around. Before we were joined in the noisy ports of call by his party-loving comrades, I spent long hours alone with him, and was pleased to glimpse new sides of him. Out at sea, my father never seemed mired in preoccupations, and minor concerns could not provoke him. When I asked about the moon's hidden sway over the tides, why the sharks we spotted looked so essentially evil yet the dolphins spun and romped in the wake of our boat, why each sundown he searched for the evening star, and why he always called the ocean "she," he not only heard my voice, my father heard my words, and he answered me eagerly and patiently.

But then, one early morning, when the sea was cobalt

blue and the coast only a long green line, my ever-changing father discombobulated me.

"When I die," he said, "I don't want to miss the ocean. I want to stay here. That's why I don't want to be buried, I want to be cremated when I die. Then take me out and scatter me over the ocean, because that's where my heart is."

My father, like that night in my bedroom, was not making any sense. Seven years old, I understood that some people die, but I'd certainly never considered that death could come for my dad. Sure, I had noted that he was much older than the fathers of all my girlfriends, but the fact had no weight. My father was not a normal man, so he could not be measured in normal terms. He personified power, and even the thinnest possibility of his death was so preposterous as to not be worth a moment of my time. His words seemed so strictly out of place, on this fine clear day, and yet stranger still was my father's expression. Though speaking of his death, he looked hopeful, even serene, wholly unlike a man who was daunted by life's limitations. In fact, I was starting to see, when our ship was underway and my father was feeling the tang of brisk, cool, salted air, there was little or nothing of life that did not excite and intrigue him.

This meant he was at his very best, and I thought the trip would be good for him. I felt confident the trip would be good for us all. Never was a confidence less justified.

13

The wickedest storm of the trip hit while we sat anchored at a Mediterrean port. I heard it first, a dull roll of faraway thunder. Then I saw lightning striking all around, lacerating the sky. Soon the thunder came in louder, sharper cracks and my parents' friends rushed to the stern. Over their heads I could see orange flames. A hillside home was burning, a man swore he had seen it struck by lightning, and a woman began to sob. Big drops of water pounded our deck and in moments everyone was wet. *The Wild Goose* spanned 136 feet, yet she rocked now like a toy boat in a rowdy child's bathtub. Whipped by the new moon, the ocean crashed inside our living room. When the sea rose again and drenched our downstairs cabin, all the adults looked nervously to my father. Even some of the highly capable crew stood frozen in place, no one assuming leadership. The sobbing woman then became hysterical. "I've never been out in lightning! My God! I've never been out in it!" She chanted this over and over, until I felt vexed almost beyond the point of endurance. I knew she couldn't, but I felt like screaming "Stop!"

My father went to her then. He didn't touch her, and I couldn't make out his words through the heavy darkness and rain. She quit her sobbing, though, and soon started giggling in a high-pitched girlish tone. Several adults started laughing with her, and even one of the men made light of his own fear. The rain still fell in earnest, but the lightning strikes had receded and the storm appeared in retreat.

It wasn't. Later that evening the black clouds burst again. Though the sea stayed out of our ship, it battered her sides on and off through the night. By the time my father and I rose with the sun to survey the damage, the winds had died and the sea had flattened. The adults appeared topside around nine, looking puffy-faced and drowsy, but by mid-afternoon they had drunk, gambled, regained their vim. I could tell by their manner and conversation that they were pleased with themselves, as if the night before they had passed some collective test. I was pleased with my father, who had quietly shared his mettle.

I had never seen my father so flustered. What the savage storm couldn't do, Grace Kelly could.

With our ship moored in Monte Carlo, my father had planned a rare early night. I think he was still worn out by the visit of the William Holdens, who had just flown back to their home in Nairobi, Africa. My dad was extremely fond of Bill Holden, but from the moment they'd stepped on *The Wild Goose,* he and his wife Ardis had bickered nearly nonstop. Apparently Mr. Holden's marriage was not holding together, and a heavy drinker anyway, he started binging. Though not in the habit of imbibing day and night, my father and his old friend drank steadily for the better part of two weeks. When my father drank in front of me, he was prone to act sloppier, sillier, more gregarious, never mean, but sometimes obnoxious. When Mr. Holden drank he seemed not to change at all: unerringly kind to everyone else, he fought constantly with his spouse.

Between the boozing and the tension between his guests, when the Holdens left my father sought little more than a private night with my mom in their master bedroom. But that night my parents were first disturbed by me—I couldn't sleep and crept to their bedroom—and several hours later by a member of our crew. "It's Princess Grace!" he announced. "It's Princess Grace! She's coming on board!"

It was after midnight. Running to the mirror, my father said "Jesus!" Though sleeping soundly I woke up quickly, desperately wanting to meet Princess Grace. My parents had met her earlier at a party hosted by movie mogul Jack Warner, honoring her engagement to Prince Rainier, when Grace Kelly was leaving Hollywood. I, on the other hand, had seen her only on TV and in my mother's magazines. Even there, her fresh pure skin looked aglow. She was the most radiant woman I'd ever seen, and I yearned to see her in person. My hopes were dashed by my father. "It's very late," he said in a tone with no room for rebuttal. "You're a little girl, and we're in a hurry."

A hurry? He was positively rattled. Rushing to peel off his pajamas, his thick fingers fumbling at little buttons, he finally cursed and quit in exasperation. While my mother lagged behind a little longer, John Wayne marched out to greet the Princess of Monaco wearing his silk pajamas hidden beneath his clothes.

Several days later, in Portofino, still feeling pouty over not meeting my first authentic princess, it barely registered when my father was called to work. Henry Hathaway was prepared to shoot *Circus World,* so we flew directly to Madrid, where my parents had rented a villa belonging to Ava Gardner. During their tempestuous affair, Miss Gardner had shared this home with Frank Sinatra. Now, behind the actress' villa, an unheated pool was cracked and dirty, and squawking chickens tromped through Ava Gardner's tomatoes. I found it kind of neat, and bohemian; hating it, my mother called it "barely livable." Already working long hours for Henry Hathaway, my father did not seem to care either way. Exhausted, all he wanted at night was food and a bed.

It was only a few days later that my father and I were mobbed near Madrid. Despite this trauma, I don't recall hearing my parents discuss it. Then again, they were not talking much about anything. I could tell they were not getting along well; I wanted to go home. But our trip was still young, the mobbing only prelude to the nightmare.

14

The least of my family's problems, *Circus World* itself was well on its way to failure. In 1963, Rita Hayworth was only forty-five, but her once-soaring career was in decline. My father had never worked with her, and never hoped to again. A consummate professional, he did not comprehend why a veteran actress arrived chronically late, without knowing her lines, only to start acting surly to peers. Alienating him further, when he and my mother dined out with Miss Hayworth near the onset of filming, she was nasty and condescending to waiters and busboys. That was anathema to my father. "Never lose the common touch," he told me throughout my life. "Never think anyone is better than you, but never assume you're superior to anyone else. Try and be decent to everyone, until they give you reason not to."

My father's opinion of Rita Hayworth notwithstanding, neither he nor his leading lady tried keeping their children from playing together. While our parents made bad chemistry on-screen and off, I cavorted on the sidelines with Rita's young daughter, Yasmin. Near the end of her mother's life, when Miss Hayworth tragically got Alzheimer's disease, it was Yasmin who put her own life on hold to caretake her mother.

Late that November, as filming lagged on and on, we learned that someone had shot President Kennedy. In Spain, even more so than back in America, the early reports were conflicting, making it unclear whether Kennedy was dead or only wounded. When the confusion finally abated, we heard the sickening truth: John F. Kennedy was assassinated. That we were not home to experience our shock and grief with other Americans only made this obscenity more disturbing.

I have been told that my father had great dislike for all the Kennedy men, but the only ill will I witnessed myself was toward Teddy. Even before Chappaquiddick in 1969, my father watched Ted Kennedy on TV and branded him a liar and a phony. "This guy says he only cares about issues. Bullshit. He cares about getting power, and he'll say and do whatever he has to to get it—just like every other politician. If he'd just admit he's like everyone else. Ted Kennedy's so fake he makes me sick."

After the opaque events of Chappaquiddick, my father was incredulous then outraged. An evening news junkie, a religious reader of *Time* and *Newsweek,* he habitually groused at the curious predilections of certain public servants, but until Chappaquiddick I'd never seen him so worked up. One night after dinner, watching yet another report, my father went ballistic.

"Jesus Christ, it's a cover-up!" he ranted. "Anyone else would at least get indicted! They're letting him off because he's a Kennedy. That family's got too much goddamn pull!" As the televised story continued, I could see my father becoming hotter and hotter. He snatched a metal paper-weight, hurling it straight at Ted Kennedy's visage, shattering our expensive TV. My father, I surmised, was not a rational man when it came to the senator from Massachusetts.

If John Wayne bore such animus for Ted's older brother Jack, he never revealed it to me. Although he deplored his politics, although he voted for Nixon, my father gave JFK high marks for presidential leadership. After John Kennedy's sudden and senseless murder, my parents were more forlorn than I'd seen them in years.

We were all depressed and displaced. We needed to finish this movie, go home to California, and the balm of familiar surroundings. Instead we were still abroad, living in rented quarters, on a trip that now seemed doomed.

Late one night in my bed, yawning and tired but unable to sleep, I heard angry sounds emanating through the wall separating my room from my parents'. They were fighting. I was unprepared—back then their fights were still infrequent—and this only heightened my terror. In the past when they had fought, my father had done the shouting, my mother had lapsed into sullen, silent indifference. Though my mother knew she could not compete with his volume, her silence had not been submissive. She knew nothing annoyed my father more than when people simply ignored him.

Now, my mother was screaming back, and the sound through the wall kept building and building. My father sounded malicious, out of control. He was swearing, the first time I'd heard him cursing my mother. For the only time in my life I feared he might strike her.

I lay there flinching, obsessively hugging Ava Gardner's pillow, hating my life, wishing that I was in my own bed. In my bedroom at home, during my parents' rare bad fights like this one, I sometimes imagined I was elsewhere. I pretended now I was way up in the moonglow, vaulting from star to star. But I kept missing the star by inches, and my brakes were not working. Dropping through space again and again faster and faster, I kept falling back to my parents' hostile voices. Finally they stopped yelling, and I sat in the darkness taking deep breaths until the hours got small and I fell asleep.

In the morning my parents were shy around me, feeling me out to see how much I'd heard. My father lit another cigarette and the smoke curled up around him. "We're starting back home soon, babe," he said. "Just a few more weeks of shooting, then we're starting home." I nodded, leaving him coughing there in the kitchen.

I wasn't allowed on the set for the final days of shooting. The *Circus World* script called for a hazardous, spectacular, pyrotechnic climax. Playing an American cowboy and circus owner barnstorming through Europe with his troupe, my father would be caught inside his big tent as it went up in flames. The action called for him to rescue the caged animals and spectators by chopping down seats and poles with an axe, setting up a fire barrier. As usual, my father chose to perform his own stunt in this critical scene, feeling he owed that to his fans, who went to John Wayne movies expecting credibility. For five straight days my father ate smoke, from artificial fires and real fires, set and put out and set again. "I'll be fine," he promised my mother each night. "Once the fire scene is finished I'll be fine. This is what they pay me for."

The last day of shooting in Spain, my father's penchant for working and working and working, until he heard the word *cut,* could have killed him. Wearing fireproof underwear, a fireman's helmet beneath his hat, and wielding an axe, he began chopping his seats and poles, working close to the fire. An unexpected breeze fanned the blaze even closer to his turned back. Fragments of glowing wood swirling around him, he kept swinging his axe through the black smoke, rather than do the dangerous take again. He could not see that everyone else had fled, including Henry Hathaway, his director, as the fire exceeded their control. Assuming John Wayne would run, too, no one screamed "Cut!" and my father stayed where he was, he and the fire, until he could not withstand the smoke and heat. Seeing that he was alone, he angrily chucked down his axe and raced from the blistering tent.

That night, my father stormed in with the red-streaked eyes of a drunkard, but he hadn't been drinking. He barely spoke and until I fell asleep I heard him viciously coughing.

Shortly after, we flew to London, where the filmmakers shot some exterior scenes, then from London to Acapulco, where *The Wild Goose* and its crew had motored ahead according to plan. Our wretched vacation nearing its end, all that remained, we thought, was a simple cruise north to Newport Beach. But tragedy struck off the southernmost tip of Baja. On their night off, four of our crewmen rowed our ship's fourteen-foot skiff into Cabo San Lucas. One was Eduardo Duran Zamora, twenty years old, a fabulous athlete and effortless swimmer. I loved Eduardo Zamora. With my father's permission and trust, Eduardo had taught me how to water ski when I was only three.

By sunrise he and the other crewmen hadn't returned. All that nervous morning I could not shake my feeling that something had gone horribly wrong. That afternoon, we learned three men had drowned. Really, all three were boys, the oldest among them just twenty-four. After drinking all night at a Cabo San Lucas Fiesta, they had started back for *The Wild Goose,* their skiff overturned, and they tried swimming the two miles to shore. The sole survivor was the only one who couldn't swim, Efran, our houseman Fausto's son. Efran had lashed himself to the skiff and been rescued by the crew of a passing boat.

As *The Wild Goose* started home my mind was mostly blank. When I thought at all, I could not accept Eduardo's death. He swam like the fish, he even taught the adults things—now he was gone? Forever?

A blanket of gloom settled over my father as well. Except for meals, he spent most of the next few days high up at the bow, in front of the glass shielding the captain. When he did come down my father looked sick with self-reproach. The boys had drunk too much beer and tequila, and the deep black sea had taken them. But I think my father held himself

responsible. All his abilities to lead, to protect, all his meticu-
lous planning, and now three of his crew were dead. I desperately wanted to give my father some comfort, to take him in
my arms and say Things will get better, Daddy, they always
do. But I wasn't sure they would, and I wasn't sure my father
would let me.

15

Just ten weeks after my family returned from our European disaster, we left for Hawaii. Kirk Douglas, Patricia Neal, and my father were starring in *In Harm's Way,* directed by Otto Preminger. To Hollywood's surprise, my father and Mr. Preminger had no blow-ups. Mr. Preminger, like Alfred Hitchcock, was a self-admitted hater of actors. While directing other pictures, he'd tried overpowering Frank Sinatra, Marilyn Monroe, and Lee J. Cobb. I knew that would never happen with my dad. Unless he was working with John Ford, my father would never be bullied by any director, or even lectured to. Having plied his craft by then for thirty-plus years, having worked again and again with not only Ford but Howard Hawks, my father felt his comprehension of cinema far transcended the standard actor's. In fact, he was certain he understood moviemaking more deeply than many of his directors. As he told the *Los Angeles Times,* "I've worked with directors who couldn't walk across the street without help."

To everyone's relief, he and Mr. Preminger earned each other's respect. While I played with Mr. Preminger's twins, our fathers behaved like perfect gentlemen. The only edginess I saw in Hawaii was between my parents. My father had never really stopped coughing since we left Spain. Even in the crystalline air of Hawaii, it became so torturous that some days he had to stop shooting his scenes. As she'd been doing for weeks, my mother insisted he see a physician; my obstinate father said no.

Before making *In Harm's Way,* my dad had gone to the Scripps Clinic in La Jolla for the mandatory physical all stars had to pass to qualify for the expensive insurance movie companies carried for them. Since the well-respected Scripps staff pronounced him suitably healthy, he did not plan to return until late in the fall of 1964, in order to be cleared for *The Sons of Katie Elder.* Things changed when Mr. Preminger wrapped up *In Harm's Way* early. Returning to Encino a few weeks before expected, during those broiling days of August my mother nagged my father into acquiescence.

Agreeing to move up the date of his next exam, my father drove south for La Jolla alone, in his customized Pontiac station wagon with the raised roof over the driver's head and its special GM engine with 350 horsepower. My father adored that car, and drove it like he, and it, would last forever. Whenever we saw him sliding behind the wheel, instead of George Coleman who sometimes drove for him, my mother and I refused to sit in the front. Considering himself a terrific driver, my father brazenly zipped through traffic while my mother and I sat in back with our hands locked in death grips. He only drove slowly on our Sunday rides through the San Fernando Valley, when we had no destination, our only goal to try and relax.

That August morning, too, I suspect my father stopped

racing and took his time. Between Encino and La Jolla, long stretches back then were still undeveloped, the road winding south astride jutting cliffs and crying seagulls, curving golden beaches and white-capped turquoise water. God, how my father loved the California coastline. Besides, he was driving to a hospital, and in his fifty-eight years he had learned to hate them. He always said he hated the loss of privacy most of all, but he also loathed the bottles and tubes and needles and blipping machines.

This time they kept my father at Scripps for five days, probing, draining, injecting, inserting, and possibly saving his life. Because something inside his body was out of control.

16

That September 1964, a tumor approximating the shape and size of a golf ball was detected on my father's smoke-damaged lung. There was little question what caused it. As my father said, "When I started smoking I was just a kid."

From the day he began, sometime during the 1920s, my father smoked cigarettes in earnest. During an addiction spanning four decades, he rarely consumed less than three packs a day, or more than six. When diagnosed with lung cancer, his habit was five packs daily. Always my father smoked Camel nonfilters: high tar, high nicotine.

A chain-smoker to the extreme, he used one match a day to spark the morning's first cigarette. Until he slept that evening, my father lit the rest with the one he was just finishing.

At the house in Encino, our ashtrays overflowed with bashed, wormy white butts. As are most heavy smokers, my father was Pavlovian: when the telephone rang and it was for him, he immediately lit a cigarette. He loved smoking. It was part of his identity. He even had his own distinctive mannerism. Most people held their cigarettes higher, just above their knuckles. My father held his deep inside the cleft of his fingers, close to his palm. When he puffed, his huge hands obscured the whole bottom of his face. "See," he would say, "other people smoke this way. Except *I* smoke like this."

My father had large appetites. In those days, when he wasn't in front of the camera, I rarely saw him without a cocktail, a cigarette, some food. Today we know that one key to a healthy life is moderation. Moderation was never attractive to my father. Jimmy Stewart once described him as having "the enthusiasm for life that would make a high school football star envious." My father loved that quote, and I think he took it to heart. He may have turned the corner of middle age, may have been through many travails, but he still thought of himself as that young jock, still indulging his youthful habits long after it was physically prudent. He knew he smoked much too heavily, at times overdrank, but he was still John Wayne, the Duke, America's emblem of manhood—nothing could touch him. In the two weeks between his diagnostic visit to Scripps and his scheduled surgery at Good Samaritan Hospital, I never saw my dad without a cigarette in his hand. Part of that, I'm sure, was his body craving tobacco, a substance with a grip as merciless as heroin. Part of it was probably this: *If I do have cancer, why stop now? It's a little late after forty years.* And part of the mixture was hubris, my immortal-feeling father saying "screw you" to his disease.

Besides, my father believed much more deeply in luck than he ever did in doctors or medicine. One afternoon before we'd left for Spain, we'd been walking along a sidewalk in the Valley and I'd veered toward the curb, to walk it like a tightrope as children will. When a light pole came between us, my father said, "Bread and butter." He explained as I started asking: "Anytime we have to walk around different sides of things, I have to say bread and butter. Or you do. Otherwise we'll stay divided." Although he smiled when I did, my father looked every bit serious.

As a girl I delighted in his superstitions, for they made him seem childlike, like me, and because sharing his quirky beliefs was a rite, and rites with my father I never passed up. Now that I'm older, I wonder about them sometimes, about their hold over him. Was he trying to distance himself from death, in the only way he deigned to? Because if good luck could enhance a man's life, surely bad luck could end it. And so for years while my father drank tequila, smoked Camels, and later smoked thin cigars, even after getting lung cancer, he opened umbrellas outside, refused salt unless it was placed on the table, circled his chair three times when a poker card flipped upright, and threw apoplectic fits at the sight of a hat on a bed. Just about his whole life, my father was willing to defy medical science. Yet he was never so bold as to challenge the fates.

During his first battle with cancer, no one sat me down and explained that he *had* cancer. My parents, I'm sure, knowing an eight-year-old child can only intellectualize so much, did not want to scare me and burden me, did not want the notion of my father's death to even enter my mind. As far as I can recall, my dad and I never once spoke of his illness. When I asked my mother why Daddy was going to the hospital, she said my father was ill, he was having an operation, but he was fine. Whenever she left me to go to Good Samaritan, I'd rearrange drawers, play with dolls I'd outgrown, pass time any way I could, but I was never able to lose my feelings of resentment, fear, and confusion. Why was no one giving me real explanations? Why was no one telling me the whole story? It made me mad then, but I don't blame either one of my parents. Even now, with so much more available information, when families discover cancer they often don't tell one another the truth.

We were all making believe. When the spot on his lung was first identified, my father told my mom he probably had "valley fever." The two jittery weeks before his biopsy, my family engaged in an unspoken conspiracy of denial. Smoking harder than ever, my father was a whirlwind, taking almost no rest and laboring long hours over a national television spot he planned doing for Barry Goldwater. Meanwhile, I voiced none of my anxieties, and did not ask any penetrating questions. Even when I was not in the room, my mother says she and my dad discussed the election, the Dodgers, the cold war, the weather, everything but my father's serious predicament. Neither one of them ever said the word *cancer.*

I suppose they couldn't bring themselves to. In 1964, as the newspapers printed advance reports of the surgeon general's imminent report on heavy smoking, Americans got confirmed what they grimly suspected: a diagnosis of lung cancer was practically a death sentence. Even today, lung cancer's five-year survival rate is only 13 percent, regardless of what stage the cancer is in when detected. Lung cancer still kills more than 140,000 Americans a year, recently making it the leading cause of cancer deaths among both women and men. Stricken with lung cancer, and given how hard he smoked, my father surviving five years was unusual. Living another fifteen, and performing in eighteen more movies, bordered on supernormal.

My father, the fighter, was gurneyed into surgery on September 17, 1964. My mother and my older brothers and sisters, by then adults, gathered in the waiting room while I was at school. The malignant growth on his left lung was so large the surgeon had to enter through my dad's back, affording him fuller view of any tentacles that might have grown out from the tumor. After the doctor removed two ribs on his left side and the entire upper lobe of his left lung, my father awoke to find he had one functioning lung.

The price, while very high, could have been final. Although malignant, the cancer had not yet metastasized: the murderous cells had not broken away from the tumor and spread through his lymph or blood systems. It had taken them six hours, but the doctors were calling the operation a triumph. There had not been complications, a Dr. Jones told my mother. Her husband had "come through it in good shape."

My mother asked if her husband's cancer was "cured."

"These things aren't cut and dried," Dr. Jones said. "I removed all the cancer, but we don't call it a 'cure' for five years. If the cancer doesn't recur, there's no reason why your husband can't live a relatively normal life."

At hearing "relatively normal" my mother says she wanted to scream.

I felt like screaming a few days after the surgery. Finally allowed to visit my father, at the eleventh hour I was not admitted to his room. Like many moments regarding my father's first cancer, I cannot recall this one vividly. I don't recall who stopped me, the nurses or my mother. All that comes back to me now is my racking worry for my dad, my helplessness, and most of all my rage. He was right *there,* on the other side of the door, and someone again was pushing me into darkness.

Several years later I learned what happened. The night before my aborted visit, there had, after all, been complications. Edema had distended my father's face to elephantine proportions, swelling his right eyelid until it covered both eyes and part of his forehead. In this condition someone, correctly, did not want me to see him.

Five days after his first operation, my fifty-eight-year-old dad went back into surgery. As they drained the accumulation of fluid from the edema, and treated both his severed stitches and the damaged tissue surrounding his mutilated lung, this time the procedure lasted six and a half hours. Following this second operation, my father drifting in and out of sedation, another thread of despair ran through his ordeal. He learned that his brother had lung cancer too.

Uncle Bob was around us a lot. Whatever contentious feelings my father once had for his younger brother, it seemed to me he had reconciled them. If I'm right about this, it speaks well of my dad. As a child, forever hearing his mother say "Bobby this" and "Bobby that," he had felt like the older, unwanted sibling. By the time both boys became men, their father had died and their mother had remarried. When my father found stardom, virtually every week he received a call from his mother posing a similar question: "What are you doing for Bobby?"

For both her and his little brother, John Wayne was doing a lot. In a way that I knew was heartfelt, my dad often spoke to me about "second chances," how everyone deserved "at least one." For all his macho preening, forgiving was intrinsic to my dad's nature. Though unwilling or unable to ever forget his childhood, he understood that life is too special a thing to be spent in recrimination.

Instead, John Wayne persuaded industry friends to give his brother jobs. He put Uncle Bob on the payroll at Batjac, and bailed him out of financial quagmires. Unlike his ambitious older brother, my Uncle Bob was not self-driven. Chatty and charming, Uncle Bob was also smaller and less imposing than my father, consistent while he was mercurial, opportunistic while he was steadfast, drawn to the glitz of Hollywood while my father cared about filmmaking. Other than some facial resemblance, all Uncle Bob and my father ostensibly shared was a weakness for steak and cigarettes. But my father's brotherly love was easy for us to see.

Uncle Bob would not survive the five years, lung cancer victim's supposedly critical juncture. He would die in 1970, after my father returned from filming *Rio Lobo,* Howard Hawks' final picture. Not long before Uncle Bob's death, my father took me to see him in the hospital. On the otherwise quiet ride over, once my father spoke harshly, "You know what your uncle did? He's got a tube in his throat, and the stupid sonofabitch is inhaling cigarettes through *that.*"

When we entered Uncle Bob's room, the torpid air had the odor of illness. I was thirteen years old; looking at my uncle, looking into the eyes of his wife, I understood he would die soon. When my father saw his gaunt, grayed younger brother, his anger at Uncle Bob, at cancer, at life and at death, blew away like a summer storm. We all smiled and hugged and gossiped and teased—my father and his brother teased each other a lot—then we left so my uncle could rest. The last time I saw my sweet Uncle Bob, he was fighting with his wife, demanding cigarettes.

17

Early that October 1964, my father came home pale and wan, the life whipped out of him by two major surgeries. Over the years, the unyielding assault of cigarette smoke on the cells lining his bronchial tubes had enlarged other mucus-secreting cells. A full, healthy breathing apparatus can cleanse itself to some extent, but with one lung removed and the other harmed by smoke, my father found breathing a constant and frightening struggle. Some days he sounded like he was choking on phlegm.

He placed most of the blame on his high-priced doctors, however. "I've only got one lung," he kept complaining, "and the damn doctors go and twist my windpipe. They twisted it on their goddamn way out. How the hell is a man supposed to breathe with one lung and a twisted windpipe?"

Those first tenuous days he would mostly lie in bed, staring at the ceiling. I would catch glimpses of him as I walked by his open bedroom door, wondering when he would show me the scar. He had promised to let me see it as soon as he stripped off his heavy abdominal bandage. I awaited this with a mixture of trepidation and curiosity, and then one night he summoned me into his room. Purple and raised and violent, the scar ran from his left breast, swinging beneath his armpit, back up to his left shoulder blade. I didn't mean to wince but I was alarmed. I realized only then how deeply my father had been in trouble.

After initially hiding his cancer, in late December my father called a press conference to tell the country the truth. For several weeks he and his managers had carefully misled the public, distributing phony releases, for fear of the cancer tainting my father's career. It was not so much his fans he was worried about, but the Hollywood men who employed him.

"I'll never work again if they find out how sick I am," he said over and over that long grim autumn. "If they think an actor is sick they just won't hire him." But first came the gossip and rumors, then the inquiries from the press, and my father saw he could no longer live out a lie. Four days after Christmas, he stood in front of our living room, packed with buzzing reporters.

"They told me to withhold my cancer operation from the public because it would hurt my image," he started, *they* meaning his advisors. I knew that was not entirely forthright, since he'd been in full agreement, and since no one made John Wayne do what he himself did not want to. It was also the first time, and the last, I ever heard my father say the word *cancer.* Even fourteen or fifteen years later, when my father got cancer again, around me he would only call it "the Big C."

"Here's what *I* believe," my father continued to tell the press. "Isn't there a good image in John Wayne beating cancer? Sure, I licked the Big C." As the stunned reporters scribbled their notes, my father announced he was leaving for Mexico next month, to star with his old friend Dean Martin in *The Sons of Katie Elder.*

The reporters filed out to work on what they knew would be major stories. My mother looked nonplussed, having pleaded with my dad to take far more time off than this. Exhausted, my father vanished upstairs and into his bedroom, back to his hospital bed by the wall, and the two green tanks of bottled oxygen. I returned to my own room, visualizing the gruesome scar, wondering how he could possibly ride a horse after doctors had cut him wide open. The first week of the new year, fourteen weeks after losing one rib and half of his lung, my father packed his bags and went south of the border.

18

Durango sits high in the mountains of Mexico, a languid, lonesome village some eight thousand feet above sea level at the eastern edge of the Sierra Madres. Immediately my father loved it—its hard blue skies and clear mountain air—but to me the place looked deadly dull. Durango had frozen dirt streets with no names, one horseshoe-shaped hotel, and one hole in the wall that everyone called a diner. A pampered product of Southern California, I took one look at my new home for the week and began counting the days.

At least Dean Martin was there. If any of my father's friends could perk up Durango it had to be him. My dad never ran with the rest of the Rat Pack, but he and Mr. Martin really did enjoy one another. Perhaps Mr. Martin wore another face when he was alone with his own family, but whenever I saw him he seemed entirely secure inside his own skin. He had a zest for living, a carefree air about him that enlivened my father whenever they hung around. I never saw rivalry between them, or competition, or jealousy, or any need to impress. Back in Southern California, they often secured Hollywood movies before their release, then screened them at our house with my mother and Jeanne Martin. Those nights there was always a lot of laughter, a lot of cheerful noise.

On the set of *Katie Elder,* the two Hollywood stars did more than their share of drinking. Late, late one night the week I was in Durango, I was jolted awake by a racket outside our hotel room. Stumbling outside I saw cast, crew, writers, and paparazzi standing outside their own rooms waving and grinning. Down below in the dirt street, my father and Dean Martin marched arm-in-arm, singing their booze-soaked lungs out. I laughed because everyone else did, but I wasn't sure I thought it was all that funny. My father was still a sick man.

Around the time my dad turned sixty, after we'd moved to Newport Beach, he cut his drinking back sharply. But in 1965, he was still being described as "one of Hollywood's legendary drinkers." Henry Fonda, after hitting Mexican bar after bar with John Ford and my father, said "John Wayne can outdrink any man." I suspect my father took pride in that assessment. To men of his generation, the ability to drink hard was certification of manhood, and my father never shrank from demonstrating his own. He liked whiskey, but his favorite drink was straight tequila on ice, and always Commemorativo. He used to take his own bottle with him to parties, bestow it on the bartender with a generous tip, and tell him or her, "Here you go. This is what I drink. Pour this for me all night." If my father met a person he liked, found that person engaging in the area of politics or moviemaking, he might sit with his new friend and smoke and drink for three straight days. After his companion left, though, he might not touch liquor for a month. My father enjoyed liquor's effects. When he drank, he was apt to make it count. But alcohol never controlled his life.

A stickler on the issue of drinking and driving, his favorite place to indulge was on *The Wild Goose.* Sometimes the horseplay got out hand. Once, I've been told, my parents docked for the weekend off Catalina Island, while entertaining Claire Trevor Bren and her husband-manager Milton. In 1939, Claire starred with my dad in John Ford's *Stagecoach,* playing Dallas the softhearted hooker to my father's Ringo Kid. Claire remained very close with my dad, as did her husband Milton Bren, a small, caustic intellectual whom my father found amusing despite this odd fact: Milton Bren loved ridiculing John Wayne. This moonlit night on *The Wild Goose,* Milton started again on my father. By then my dad had had quite a few, and more than enough. Unzipping his pants, he turned on the jabbering Bren and urinated all over his shoes. As the story goes, for the first time in his life Milton Bren fell speechless.

I never saw my father so plainly smashed, and when he drank around me he was never abusive. On the contrary, there was a sweetness about him, an approachability—and that's what annoyed me. He was *always* like that with his friends, and yet frequently closed or distracted around his children. Even before I understood liquor, I intuitively knew his mood change was unnatural. I wanted him to be open without drinking booze.

One of my worst and earliest memories of my father's drinking is the Encino morning when I started leaving for school and he and his buddies were still embroiled in the same game of poker they'd played all night. I still remember John Ford's stubbled, scowling face, one black eyepatch over black-framed glasses, gnawing the end of a fat cigar in the corner of his mouth. I don't recall much about Mr. Ford, except he was always gentle with me, and I thought of him as my grandpa. But Mr. Ford also scared me. With that black eyepatch, he reminded me of death.

Nor did my father look too spry that bloodshot morning.

There were maybe six loud men in our smoky card room, still puffing away and drinking, but even the wisecracks and clinking of glasses could not muffle my father's thundering order.

"Hey Aissa! Give me a kiss before you go to school!"

Obediently, I pecked my father's cheek. He wetly kissed me back on my own, and that's when I smelled it. His whiskey breath smelled hot and stale. It smelled obnoxious.

Because of my father's capacity to drink, because every morning when he was away on location he showed up first on a film set, wholly prepared for the day's opening shot while his fellow drinkers lurched in looking pathetic, missing their marks, and blowing their lines, he was widely described by journalists as a man immune to getting hungover.

Nonsense.

When only his family could see him, his heart pounded so vehemently some mornings my father swore he was having a heart attack.

"My heart, my heart," he'd bitch and yell. "Pilar, I'm gonna die. Pilar, where are you? Goddamn it! I will *never* drink again. Pilar!"

There was plenty of drinking that freezing week in Durango, and plenty of showboating by my father in front of the press. He wanted the world to believe he was still the invincible Duke, and clearly no sick and faltering man. As for the photographers and reporters, I'm sure some came to Durango for simply professional reasons—my father was news—and that many were pulling for his revival. Others, I think, came morbidly hoping to witness John Wayne's demise. A few days before I left Durango, the ghoulish nearly got what they came for.

This January morning, while filming a pivotal fight scene, my father would be pulled from his horse, land in a mountain stream, then engage in a lengthy brawl with his three "brothers." But the stream was ringed with ice, the weather near 10 degrees. Afraid my father could get pneumonia, my mom asked if he'd please use a double. My fool-hardy father said no: the director, Henry Hathaway, was shooting the scene in close-up.

Mr. Hathaway yelled "Action." On cue, my father got yanked into the stream. But he landed wrong, getting drenched to the waist instead of just to his knees. Horrified, my little brother Ethan yelled "Daddy, Daddy." Henry Hathaway shot Ethan a glare and continued shooting. Chilled to the bone, operating on one good lung, my father completed the scene, but trudging out of the water he couldn't stop coughing. His body convulsed and his lips turned a rubbery grayish-blue. The photographers closed in and took their pictures. Henry Hathaway, suddenly now my father's protector, screamed "Get away, you sons of bitches! Can't you see he needs air?" An aide rushed up with my father's inhalator, fixing the oxygen mask over his ashen face.

The crisis passed, but I was still trembling. And angry.

My father is still in poor health. Why can't he stop confirming his courage? Is he such a prisoner of his myth he'll feed it at the risk of his very life?

I didn't know, but the questions entered my mind as we all stood around watching my father breathe.

19

After we'd all returned to the states, my father surprised me one evening at dinner. "Your mother and I," he said, "are thinking of moving to Newport Beach, not far from where the boat is. We want to know what you think. Would you like to move to Newport?"

For me it was easy. Partial to the cool climes of the beach, weary of living a life on a hill behind ten-foot walls, pleased that my father was solicitous of my feelings on such an important matter, I told him yes, moving sounded wonderful. In May 1965, having closed the sale of our estate to Walt Disney's eldest daughter, I had scant regret and great hope as we left behind our past for a future by the sea.

Before its lima bean fields were paved over with concrete, Newport Beach in 1965 was a close-knit seaside village of 36,000 people, with few markets or restaurants, so anywhere you went you ran into people you knew. The crown jewel of Orange County, Newport back then was a collection of mansions and bungalows, yachts and dinghies, ship brokers and stockbrokers, pensioned retirees and golden-haired, brown-skinned surfers. Friends visited homes of friends in sailboats and motor boats, sidling up to the slip to indulge in sunset cocktails, until eyes swam in heads like ice cubes in tall glasses. Many of these beach houses were still weekend homes and summertime havens, to which monied and stressed Los Angelenos fled south in sports cars and sedans.

Although our own new waterfront home was still being remodeled, Newport Beach seemed lovely to me even from rented quarters. The springtime scents alone were enough to make me forget Encino: misted Pacific air and rain-dampened sand, creamy freesia and Spanish blueblood, orange blossoms and night-blooming jasmine. Most exhilarating of all, after living on five and a half secluded acres, my old childhood dream had actually come true. Unlike in Encino, other children now played directly outside on the street in front of our home. My father was off in Rome filming *Cast a Giant Shadow* with Kirk Douglas, and had not yet appeared at our rented home. With none of the other children suspecting who I was, how nice it felt to be treated as just one more neighborhood girl.

That September I entered fifth grade at Carden Hall, a small conservative private school. Each grade at Carden was dissected into Upper and Lower. After our first two sets of exams I was promptly kicked upstairs to Upper Fifth. That night I was flowing with pride, waiting for my father's daily phone call home from Rome. Although I'd been nervous about my school, I'd applied myself and accomplished something worthwhile, without my father's assistance. Knowing what emphasis he placed on grades, I was sure he'd be thrilled.

"Dad, I skipped lower fifth grade!" I said over the line. "My tests were so good my teachers moved me up!"

"What's so great about that?" my father replied. "Why didn't you skip the whole grade?"

"I don't know, Daddy. I just thought . . ."

"Next time skip the whole grade."

Closing the subject, he asked for my mother. All I wanted was a little approbation. Instead I slinked to my bedroom crushed, never to mention it to him again.

When my father came home that fall we were all much more relaxed. The stress of remodeling behind us, we were relieved to finally move into our new home, a one-story, ten-room, seven-bath white ranch house with a pool, sitting right at the tip of Bayshore Drive, a plush subdivision in Newport. Although the front of our house could only be approached through a gated, guarded entrance, it was far less private than the hilltop house in Encino. Even in 1965, Newport waterfront property was at a premium and homes were jammed shoulder to shoulder on narrow plots of land. Despite the loss of privacy, my father loved our new house, especially our new patio. Built on a jutting point, it afforded a vast, spectacular view of Balboa Island, Lido Island, and foremost, the bay, with its channels of green and blue and hazel waters. Every chance he could, my dad sat outside and inhaled his sea-kissed surroundings. He felt so comfortable out in our yard, he remained unfazed even when the Balboa Island ferry cruised by, affording its shutter-happy tourists an intimate view of John Wayne.

My father seemed satisfied with his new life, but my own was about to radically change. Upon my dad's return from Rome, word spread that John Wayne had purchased a home in Newport. After that, seemingly overnight, going to school became catastrophic. In the halls, in class, at recess, my schoolmates now constantly watched me. The rare times I looked anyone in the eye, I saw envy, resentment, suspicion. Most of my new classmates had lived in Newport all their lives and grown up with one another. I was the stranger. Not only the stranger, but "John Wayne's daughter," obliterating any chance I might have had of hanging back and gradually shedding my status as an outsider. I felt wildly conspicuous. The more my peers stared and pointed and sneered, the more drastically I turned inward. "The only way for people to think you're a jerk," my father had trained me, "is for you to open your mouth." Avoiding conversations for fear of being scorned, I was quickly perceived and dismissed as a snob. It took weeks before anyone but a teacher spoke directly to me. Meanwhile, the whispers grew louder and more derisive, burning my ears and making me feel like a freak.

"There she is. John Wayne's daughter. She's such a bitch."

"Look at her nose, it's stuck in the air."

"She doesn't talk to anyone."

"Who does she think she is?"

Before very long, I found myself frequently blurting "I'm sorry" to my parents and my brother, Ethan, at inappropriate times when I'd done nothing wrong. Even my voice changed, from one with at least a ring of self-assurance to one conveying anguished self-doubt. I was nine years old, and I hated the timid young girl I was becoming. I knew that I should be tougher. I *wanted* to be. But my coddled past had left me soft at the edges.

I finally turned to my mother. But I didn't reveal the extent of my alienation. "Mom," I said in my tiny apologetic voice, "I'm shy now at school. I feel real shy with the other kids."

My mother said, "Ah! You're not shy! Don't ever say that again!"

That was that. If my mother did not want to listen, I had nowhere to go with my feelings. My father was out of the question: I never felt my faults were anything he and I could discuss. My father never perceived me as scared or weak, as a little girl with any emotional problems. And I felt I must live up to his notion of who I was.

So I kept my pain and fear inside, secretly detesting my new environment. For as long as I could recall, I'd always understood that my father was special. But only in the fish tank of Newport Beach did I comprehend the depth of his superstardom. Not only the children at Carden Hall, but the teachers, the parents, the entire community knew of my father's presence. Instead of cancer destroying his career and his image, it amplified them. When my father seemingly "licked the Big C" he acquired mythic dimensions. As my father's stardom advanced, it eclipsed my entire identity. Thinking about it now, I must have resented him for it, even at nine years old, and yet I recall blaming everyone else but him until my sophomore year in high school. Perhaps resenting my father was scary to me, in the face of everyone else's adoration. Perhaps I felt guilty for feeling it. So I hid it even from myself.

That first year in Newport, even my childhood dream betrayed me. Yes, the Bayshore complex teemed with children, but most were older than I, and even more affluent and noninclusive than the younger kids at my private school. The beach just behind our new house was the most threatening place of all, with its clusters of rich older teenagers. They never said a word to me, but I told myself they despised me. They *all* despise me, I thought.

One day after school, a short, olive-skinned girl approached me on one of the pathways running through Bayshore. Eyes fixed straight ahead I planned on rushing right by her.

"Hi," she said, "I'm Debbie."

Debbie Doner saved my life. At least that's how it felt. My energy level rose just from being around her, and slowly my confidence, too. Sincere and perceptive, Debbie never asked about my father, unless it related to my father and me. Gently, without any rancor for my parents, Debbie encouraged me to think about my family life as we truly lived it. An outward, adventurous girl, Debbie had none of my newfound reticence. Soon we were screaming our throats raw at the California Angels, swishing our hair and singing along to the Beatles, sneaking out at night from her bedroom window, purely to see if we could escape detection. Alone with my best friend Debbie, I felt safe from the awkwardness and pressure I felt around nearly everyone else. When I found another girlfriend, Lea Hilgren, I was starting to almost feel human again.

Then our dog limped home with a shattered leg.

My dad, you see, had also found a faithful new comrade. Frosty, a rock-chested white Samoyed, had my father manipulated even as a puppy. Every morning my dad took his coffee and food out to our breakfast nook facing the bay, and every morning Frosty growled and pawed on the sliding glass window, demanding to be let in. My father would slide open the glass, pull out a chair, and let Frosty jump up and join him for breakfast. Mornings when I couldn't sleep, I'd climb out of bed before my father could jar me awake, and catch him feeding Frosty strips of bacon. My father would look embarrassed, almost childlike. Years later, I can still see them eating breakfast together, can still remember that scene with such sweet pleasure.

That first year in Newport, Frosty was not quite a year old when he vaulted our fence one afternoon while I was at school, running out on the ominous beach where the rich older teenagers made fun of Debbie and Lea and me whenever they saw us. When I came home from school, my mother told me Frosty had broken her leg. Frosty already had a cast on her right hind leg, and her tail was bent down behind her in utter depression. Even after I cried myself out, for several days my heart sunk each time Frosty took a tender step. Paranoid, or prescient, I asked Debbie and Lea to ask around. About a week later a girl from the complex told me she'd seen what happened, but that she would not name names.

The teenager boys saw Frosty down on the beach, the girl said. They called her name, beckoning her to come close, and the girl thought they were going to throw their Frisbee to her. A boy broke Frosty's leg with one cruel accurate throw.

I was incensed, and then frightened. Had we moved somewhere evil? Only a monster out of a nightmare would do such a thing to our dog.

I never told my family what happened, afraid of my

father's reaction. I feared he would storm the beach in a murderous rage, cursing and screaming, and what would the older boys do to me then? After that, I'd see them around the complex or down on the sand, the neighborhood teenage boys, knowing one had brutalized Frosty. I took what they did as an insult intended for me, a spiteful warning that I was still not wanted.

20

I was twelve years old when my parents stopped sleeping together.

The more silent and strained their marriage became, the more I found myself revisiting my early childhood, when even the music filling our home reinforced my parents' belief in conjugal love. As a young girl in Encino, I'd sometimes discover them dancing, swaying across the living room lost in each other and lost in the romantic sounds of their favorite crooners: Johnny Mathis, Frank Sinatra, Kaye Starr, Bobby Darin, Tony Bennett, Dean Martin, and Sammy Davis, Jr.

In front of their children back then, my parents were never ashamed to show their affection. Whenever my father returned from location, he could not get enough of my mother's caresses and kisses. Warm nights after dinner, first my father and I would stroll alone through the grounds of our estate, both holding our carved African canes that we'd brought home from the set of *Hatari!* After my father and I had walked and talked, he and my mother slipped on their fins and masks and swam twilight laps in our heated pool. On Friday and Saturday nights, when there were no Hollywood functions or parties, they often went straight from dinner to bed, sometimes as early as seven. How my parents loved their huge wooden bed, and how the Hollywood press loved writing about its vastness. A reporter in *Photoplay* described it as an "Early American settle bed built on the foundation of a tremendous Old English bench on which Yorkshire farmers had smoked more than two hundred yams at a time. It had been really modernized: arm rests on the sides which could be raised and lowered; a cigarette compartment for him; a pull-down book rack; a control panel for television, radio, several telephone lines—by just flicking a switch you could turn on the lights downstairs or even open the front gate; and a slide-out backgammon tray fitted into the head-board." The article went on to quote my mother "gayly" comparing her bed to a "football field."

As a child that bed was a powerful symbol for me, and I wrapped it in romance and dreams. Lying together in silk, my mom in her robe and he in pajamas, my parents used to read mysteries out loud, roar at Lucille Ball and Jackie Gleason, smoke their cigarettes, nibble hors d'oeuvres, and sip their martinis. I still recall snuggling between them, my mouth puckered from eating the baby onions inside their martinis. I can still shrink back into little girlhood whenever I think of those nights.

Their marriage lost its enchantment in Newport Beach. Until then, the lengthy separations intrinsic to show business marriages, their disparity in age, my father's slumping health and narrowing patience, had not yet become insurmountable. But coming to Newport Beach was my mother's idea at least as much her husband's, and I think she moved south seeking far more than a house by the ocean. After too many years hearing herself called "John Wayne's wife," too many years of hosting his friends and staving off his boredom, I think my mother wanted a life that felt like her own.

Shortly after we moved, she befriended a woman who belonged to the church of Christian Science. Still believing in God, but losing her faith in Catholicism, my mom converted a few days after she met her new companion. Since my father never entirely trusted doctors, her new religion's belief in self-healing was never an issue between them. But suddenly, after all the years, my mother could not join my dad for a drink or a smoke. Now she frequently withdrew into our guest room, needing solitude to digest her religion's complex books on positive thinking and mind over matter. In an effort to connect, my mother tried convincing my father to join her at church. Trying to show her he loved her he finally agreed. But my father had no personal use for organized religion, and could certainly not endorse one that forbade drinking or smoking. He only went once, and my mother said he fidgeted throughout the service. "I hated sitting still that long," he told her the moment they stepped outside. My father told me Christian Science was "too extreme," and wondered aloud what my mother was looking for. *Herself, Dad,* I wanted to say. *She's looking for herself. If I can see that, why can't you? Or why won't you?*

Of course, they still were at odds over his work. We moved to Newport just one year after his coughing, convulsing retreat from that frozen stream in Durango. My mother had not wanted my dad to work that soon in the first place. As she agonizingly watched, my mother said part of herself, and part of her marriage, died inside that icy stream. Perhaps she knew it was futile, but in Newport my mother kept saying, slow down, slow down. My father, whose parents had been so poor, kept replying, "We need the money."

If work and religion carried the greatest weight, by then small things divided them too. Both in Peru and in Encino, my mother had never perceived herself as athletic. The morning a girlfriend asked her to fill in at mixed doubles, my mother had never stepped onto a tennis court. That day, she discovered the joy of breaking a sweat and of pounding her anxieties into a yellow Wilson. Just as promptly as she got hooked, my father resented his wife's latest passion. Even when he was a younger and healthier man, my father's sports were football and surfing. He never jogged—back then few people did—never liked golf or tennis. Besides, tennis, like Christian Science, took my mother away from him; each time she left our house he found something to pick at her for. Usually it was her dresses.

"Are you actually going out like that?" my father grumbled, referring to her short hemline. Though for many years he dominated us both, my mother did not fear my father as I did. In response to his diatribes as she left, she stopped only long enough to explain that times had changed, that tennis dresses no longer came down past women's knees. Eventually my father accepted my mother's outfits, but I'm not sure I can say the same for her independence. At times he seemed so threatened and insecure.

By 1968, my father was sixty-one years old and most of his old friends were gone. Those still alive, like Dean Martin and John Ford, still lived an hour north in Los Angeles County. He would soon make new male friends, but my father had no way of knowing that. In 1968 my mother turned forty. Her mid-life was not without sadness, but in her forties my mother's self-confidence grew. As she became more interested in herself, her tennis, her new circle of young and churchgoing friends, she found less time to dote on her husband. More and more when he wasn't working, my father spent mornings and afternoons without her aboard *The Wild Goose,* reading scripts in the sun, chatting up the crew, catching sand dabs, then frying them up the next day for breakfast. At least in front of me, their physical contact decreased until little was left but pecks on cheeks and hands on shoulders. Meanwhile, over at my best friend Debbie's, her father still came home every night and flirted with Debbie's mom. Some nights while the Doners kissed and hugged in their kitchen, I thought about what my parents were doing. I wondered if they were talking. Were they even in the same room?

One day when I was twelve, without any confrontation or visible anger, my mother and father stopped sleeping together. My mom left all her belongings where they were, in the master bedroom and in her private dressing room. But every night, she retired to our guest room. My parents still loved each other. I'm certain of that. They still played bridge, still exchanged pleasantries, and if anything their bickering decreased.

Then why did their new arrangement fill me with such longing, a longing I could never quite define when I was twelve years old, and yet never quite get rid of? In the bed that meant so much to my family once, why was my dad sleeping alone? He was a big man, but their bed looked empty without my mother.

It was their marriage. It was their estrangement. Still, I was their daughter and hoped for some volunteered answers. My father left it unmentioned. My mother merely said she needed her sleep, and my father's heavy snoring was making that hard. Even at twelve I did not fully believe it. My father snored, loudly, throughout our entire lives. And yet I let their new situation drop. We all let it drop, thinking, perhaps, that our silence at least would let us get on with our lives. Looking back, I can see we were like so many other American families. In the Wayne house, when we felt awful we lied and said we felt fine, and when we were scared we walked around looking brave, because of that Wayne family pride, and because keeping our problems a secret—even among ourselves—was less frightening and painful than dragging them into the light and trying to solve them.

Father snored; mother needed her sleep.

21

Although film critics were rarely kind to my father until late in his life, I don't think even he was prepared for the maelstrom of bad press that whipped up around him in the tumultuous summer of 1968. Just that February, the Viet Cong had launched the Tet Offensive. By the time American and South Vietnamese troops had beaten back the surprise attack, one senator probably spoke for a large number of bewildered Americans: "What happened? I thought we were winning this war?" Four months later, the antiwar movement gaining fervor and size, my father came out with his staunchly pro-Vietnam war movie, *The Green Berets*. Predictably, the late '60s press attacked both him and the film with a vengeance.

A few years later, my father's conservative views would

intrude on my own life, as long-haired boys at my high school called me "right wing" because my last name was Wayne. But the summer I saw *The Green Berets,* I was twelve years old and my concerns were only for him. Beneath his public bravado, his self-esteem was always tender, and this was an especially difficult time. Although he fired back at his critics, referring to them as a "little clique back East" of "doctrinaire liberals," "not in touch with the American people," at home my father privately brooded. Unknown to the public, he and my mother were increasingly locking into separate lives. In his professional life, the genre my father so commanded—the Hollywood Western—was said to be nearing extinction. *The Green Berets* was getting skewered. My father still talked tough around the house; until his death that would never change. But some days perhaps even he thought: 1968 is not the best time to be John Wayne.

Then my father met Rooster Cogburn, the fictional sheriff in Charles Portis's novel, *True Grit.* When Henry Hathaway sent him an early peek at the novel while still in its galleys, my father instantly phoned my half-brother Michael, then at the helm of Batjac.

"Buy it," he said to Michael. "Don't dicker, buy it."

Though Paramount, not Batjac, wound up making *True Grit,* there was no industry doubt about which veteran actor would play the paunchy, grizzled, aging, hard-drinking Cogburn, a man at once heroic and flawed. *True Grit*'s director and my father's old friend, Henry Hathaway called my father the same day the deal was completed. "This Cogburn fellow is a man who wenches when he wants, gets drunk when he wants, and fights when he's in the mood. He's as much sinner as saint—and you, Duke, old friend, are going to play him that way." Hathaway also told him to play Cogburn broadly, as a mean old man indifferent to his appearance, and so not to bother dieting. This was like telling my dad he did not have to pay that year's federal taxes.

As he got older and less physically active, my father increasingly battled his weight, most acutely during the weeks before shooting a movie. One time he even sought medical help. I was surprised: He dreaded taking pills, resisting even aspirin during his hangovers. The pharmaceutical diet didn't last long, though. Prescribed a color-coded phalanx of pills, my father mistakenly took his morning pill—his "upper"—at night. Within minutes the speed kicked in. First he woke my mother, then pleaded with her. "Help me. I took the wrong goddamn pill," my father said. "I'll be up all night. As long as you're awake too, I might as well teach you how to play bridge." Although she had not been awake, my mother took pity. She spent the next eight hours learning her wired husband's favorite card game.

The rest of the time he lost the weight more naturally, somehow curtailing his urges to eat and drink as each new movie approached. Right after wrapping the movie, however, my father almost always gained it all back. I used to catch him late at night, padding from the refrigerator to the kitchen table in his silk pajamas, a long, hard salami in one hand, his miniature axe in the other. Salami, baloney, bacon, any kind of heavy red meat—my father craved them all. I know that eating like this was something he loved, but when I think of it now it breaks my heart. Back then, no one knew all those foods can combine to generate cancer. No one realized, either, that anything burnt is also carcinogenic. Late lunches and dinners, barbecued steaks were my father's idea of heaven; he ate every one charred nearly black.

Mornings, he sometimes concocted what he called "Milktoast." He'd toast a piece of white bread, dip it in milk, put a fried egg on the soggy toast, and drown it all with sugar. It's miraculous, really, when you put it all together—the cholesterol, the Camels, the red meat, the hard liquor—that my life-gorging father lived to be seventy-two. Most people who live as he did drop dead closer to forty.

When my father did shed weight, he always took enormous pride in announcing it to our family. "Well," he'd boom out, "this morning I'm 236!" The heaviest he'd ever get was about 260 pounds, and this usually happened between Halloween and Christmas. Every Halloween, he'd drive by himself to the Smart N' Final and load up on discounted candy, ostensibly for all the trick-or-treaters. Except he always bought all his favorites—black and red licorice, Tootsie Rolls, and especially Abba-Zabas, an orgy of toffee and peanut butter—and he'd buy enough for three Halloweens. In the weeks before Christmas I'd catch him sneaking them from a stack of candy stashed in his trophy room cabinet. Though I knew he'd regret it tomorrow, it was somehow nice seeing my father at such moments. Sneaking candy, looking over his shoulder just like the rest of us, my father seemed less formidable, in some way easier to love.

Although I appeared in four of his pictures—*The Alamo, The Comancheros, Donovan's Reef,* and *McClintock*—my roles were so brief that I've never considered myself a one-time "child actress." I was only six when *McClintock* was made in 1963, and an end came to my "career."

But my dream kept living. For the next three years, I harbored a secret wish to one day become a real actress. Acting was a bridge to my father's work, a bridge to him. I also knew at an early age that my father was special, and I felt through acting that I could be special too. I distinctly recall riding one New Year's Day in the Rose Parade, cruising in a long white convertible next to my father as thousands of people cheered us. All that adulation and affirmation: the sensation was very seductive.

From the time I was six until I was roughly nine, I yearned to act in my father's movies. But I never confided in him, possibly for fear of his rejection. For three years I heard about upcoming pictures, warned myself not to hope or care, then secretly felt depressed when I was passed by. I wondered what I'd done wrong, why he had stopped including me. Too young to understand that even minor casting is not that rudimentary, that even John Wayne cannot control every facet of every film, about the time I turned ten I let the dream die. It was clearly not going to happen.

In fall 1968, three weeks prior to shooting, an actress bowed out of her key part in *True Grit.* My father asked me to play the young girl who hires Rooster Cogburn to find her father's killer! Not just to say a couple lines and sayonara, the way it had been when I was small, but to costar with him in a full-blooded role, in a major picture I knew he believed could restore his flagging career.

Did my father mean it? He couldn't.

Could he?

"Uh, Aissa," my father said two days after he told me to start reading the script.

"Yes, Dad?"

"I'm real sorry, honey. I didn't mean to build your hopes up, but we're using another actress in the movie. Her name is Kim Darby. I'm not the director, honey. I'm really sorry."

"What?" I couldn't believe it. The dream had only just sparked again in the past two days, but for those two delicious days the dream had been dreamed sincerely.

"We're using another actress," my father said. I'm terribly sorry."

"That's okay, Dad."

What bullshit that was. I was devastated. By my own father I felt betrayed. And to make matters worse, I then had to go with my family to Mammoth Lakes, California, for part of *True Grit*'s filming. To justify my not getting the part, I wanted Kim Darby to be gorgeous and gifted and friendly. Instead I thought, This mousy, insolent girl is who they used over me? From her first day on the set, Kim Darby was brusque and rude to all. Whenever she acted in scenes with my father, I made sure I was somewhere else.

Apparently my irritation was starting to show. One night at the end of shooting, my father led me off where we could be alone, surely, I thought, to talk about us. To talk about *it.* Instead he told me a story about his eldest daughter Toni. Today Toni has eight children, and she's still a classical beauty. Tall and slender with clean perfect features, Toni also once dreamed of following her father into acting.

"Toni had wonderful talent, Aissa," my father started. "She studied drama and acted in plays in high school. She had wonderful bone structure, and she could have been a fine actress. I considered it all . . . and decided not to help her."

Inside, I was fuming. I felt sure we would talk about me.

"There's some awful people in this business," my father said. "I didn't want to see Toni get hurt. You know what I told her? I told her she should get married, and have a whole bunch of children. And that's what Toni did."

My anger faded into deep disappointment. There would be no more parts in his movies, not even any near-misses. This conversation had nothing to do with Toni. My father was telling me to forget about acting.

That night I felt wounded, not destroyed. After coming so close to getting *True Grit*—or so I'd thought—then missing out, I'd already started believing I'd lost my final chance. Today, I don't regret giving up the idea of acting. Even trying to live up to John Wayne's legacy would have meant falling drastically short, and I found the road to womanhood rocky enough without all of *that*. As for my father's role, I'm still not sure I've sorted out all my feelings. I never told him I wanted to act, so perhaps he never knew how much I once wanted it. I also believe he meant what he said that night in Mammoth Lakes, about not wanting his children injured by Hollywood. My father knew better than I the incredible odds against success, and I'm sure he wanted to shield me from all the dismissal I likely faced.

Given all that, when it came to his family working in Hollywood, I wonder if he was mostly paternalistic or mostly just chauvinistic. I can honestly understand him not encouraging me, since I never had Toni's looks or dramatic training. Perhaps because I lived beneath the same roof with my dominating father for twenty-three years—much longer than Toni—I also lacked her plucky self-assurance. But my father squelched Toni's ambitions, too, all but insisting she stick to hearth and home, even while opening

Hollywood doors for his two oldest boys, Patrick and Michael, and even his brother Bob. When I see Toni today she seems happy, very much pleased with her life. But with all that potential, I imagine our father's double standard must have hurt.

22

It's been frequently written that John Wayne was so secure in his work he never even kept track of his reviews. It isn't true. My father read practically all the major reviews. Those he did not lay eyes on himself, he had read to him over the phone by Mary St. John, his confidante and longtime secretary. As for the bad reviews, my father himself tried selling the notion they never upset him. After *The New York Times, Life* magazine, *The Washington Post,* and others had ripped *The Green Berets,* my dad told the Chicago *Sun-Times*'s Roger Ebert, "A little clique back in the East has taken great satisfaction in reviewing my politics instead of my pictures. And they've drawn up a caricature of me, which doesn't bother me: their opinions don't matter to the people who go to the movies."

In one respect that was accurate. For all its harsh no-
tices, *The Green Berets* ranked tenth among 1968's most popular movies. While the critics railed, enough "people who go
to the movies" made *The Green Berets* one of my father's
top-grossing films. But bad reviews did bother my father, or
he'd have never reacted with such emotion. "That son of a
bitch," he would howl after reading his work defiled in print.
"I've been in this goddamn business for fifty years. He's
never been in front of a camera in his life. What the hell does
he know about acting?" Oddly enough, I never heard him
berate *The New Yorker*'s Pauline Kael, although perhaps no
major critic ever panned my father so meanly or so persis-
tently. Of *Rooster Cogburn,* my father's spinoff of *True Grit,*
Ms. Kael observed, "The two principal subjects of the script's
attempts at humor are Wayne's gut and (Katharine) Hepburn's age, which is to say that the the film tries to make
jokes of what it can't hide." Ms. Kael also wrote of my father,
"It never Waynes, but it bores." That famous and clever and
nasty line must have stung him. I know it, even though he
would never admit such a thing.

When the glowing early reviews came in for *True Grit*
in the summer of 1969, only one year after the critical bar-
rage on *The Green Berets,* my father read every last one with
elation. Vincent Canby of *The New York Times* called it one
of "the year's best films, a major accomplishment." In *The
Village Voice,* Andrew Sarris, one of his biggest public admirers, wrote, "There is talk of an Oscar for Wayne after
forty years of movie acting and after thirty years of damn
good movie acting." My dad loved the Sarris review—doubly
so, I think, because it appeared in the left-leaning *Voice*—
and felt very proud of his work in *True Grit.* But early on,
and even after he won the nomination, he did not believe it
would bring him an Oscar. I was sitting next to him when he
saw *True Grit* in one of its earliest, roughest forms. Afterwards a man from Paramount told him, "Duke, this is the
one. This one's gonna get you the award." His eyes filled with
old broken hopes, my dad only nodded his head as if to say
thank you.

***

By playing Rooster Cogburn, an aging drunken lout whom Robert Duvall called "a one-eyed fat" man, and who'd bellowed back at Duvall, "Fill your hands, you son of a bitch!" my father poked humorous holes in both his professional and personal image. But even when the Eastern critics joined the applause, he felt fairly certain he'd wind up disappointed. He'd been nominated just once in his long career, for his stirring portrayal of Sergeant Stryker in *Sands of Iwo Jima.* On that night in 1949, my father lost to Broderick Crawford for *All the King's Men.* Twenty years and no nominations later, he predicted he'd once again play bridesmaid.

Along with him, Dustin Hoffman and Jon Voight were nominated for *Midnight Cowboy;* Peter O'Toole for *The Lion in Winter;* and Richard Burton for *Anne of the Thousand Days.* "At least I keep damn fine company," my father said. "But one of them is bound to win." After screening the other three movies at our home, he started leaning toward Dustin Hoffman. "His performance was so big, so brilliant," he said. "It's not my kind of picture, but I know a great actor when I see one." With its explicit violence and homosexuality, it really wasn't his kind of picture. Normally my father would never have seen it, or else stomped out on it very early. Typically, if my father screened a movie he began to perceive as "perverted"—he once told *Playboy* both *Midnight Cowboy* and *Easy Rider* fit this bill—he would storm out at the first scene he found offensive. "Why can't we get a decent movie?" my father would growl. "How can that son of a bitch make this type of crap!" It always felt clumsy for his guests and family, but at least my father never shut off the projector. Instead of playing Hollywood dictator, he'd just leave the room, allowing the rest of us to judge the movie ourselves. Most of the time, that is. When we screened *Last Tango in Paris,* my father made sure he dragged me out with him. To see the rest of that one I had to sneak out to the theatre.

Oscar night came that year on April 13, 1970. After our limo crawled its way through the black line of stretch limousines bound for the Dorothy Chandler Pavilion, I stepped

Aissa appeared in four movies with her father:
The Alamo, The Comancheros, Donovan's Reef, *and* McClintock *(1959).*

Aissa on the set of The Alamo
with movie "mom,"
Joan O'Brien (1956)

With real mom, Pilar (1959)

And with Chill Wills, dancing on her father's feet (1959)

John, Aissa, and Stuart Whitman on the set of Comancheros *(1961)*

Aissa on the set of Hatari, *in her father's chair (1964)*

With one of the wild animals she discovered in Africa (1964)

Atop a baby elephant. John later had one of these elephants delivered to the estate for Aissa's ninth birthday party (1965)

The Alamo, *John's first try
at directing. He also
starred in the movie (1959).*

John Wayne and Robert Mitchum, with their respective mothers,
on the set of El Dorado *(1965).*

In October 1964, John was released from Good Samaritan Hospital after undergoing two operations to remove a cancerous lung.

By March of 1965, John was back in action, here crawling out of the frigid water after a river fight in The Sons of Katie Elder; *the scene almost killed him.*

John as Rooster Cogburn in True Grit, *the film role that won him an Oscar for Best Actor in 1970.*

*With Barbra Streisand
at the 1970 Academy Awards.*

Wiping away a tear (1970)

Pilar and Aissa at home in Encino, taken by John himself (1962).

THE WEST COAST OF AMERICA TELEGRAPH CO., LTD.

CABLE WEST COAST

"VIA CABLE WEST COAST" TELEFONO 75220 "VIA WESTERN UNION"

LA 5

Edificio Electra
Jirón Antonio Miró Quesada 324
LIMA

CALLAO { CALLE DANIEL NIETO 199
TELEFONO 90166 SUCURSALES { MIRAFLORES, TARATA 227
HOTEL MAURY, TELF. 75600 HOTEL BOLIVAR, TELF. 35920
HOTEL CRILLON, TELF. 30987
HOTEL COUNTRY CLUB, TELF. 16400

No. 14. Sucursal Miraflores-Tarata 227

TELEGRAMA

LRC121 LOSANGELES CALIF 31 21 1028A.

MISS AISSA WAYNE MANUEL MIOTA 274 SANANTONIO MIRAFLORES LIMA.-

MY DARLING AISSA I SEND YOU A BIG HUG AND ONE FOR YOUR

MUMMY PLEASE DELIVER IT FOR ME LOVE.

DADDY.

Emp. y hora ....
N. B.—La Empresa no se responsabiliza por equivocaciones, demoras o falta de entrega (Ley Internacional).

CLASS OF SERVICE
This is a fast message unless its deferred character is indicated by the proper symbol.

WESTERN UNION
TELEGRAM
W. P. MARSHALL, PRESIDENT

SYMBOLS
DL=Day Letter
NL=Night Letter
1201 LT=International Letter Telegram

The filing time shown in the date line on domestic telegrams is STANDARD TIME at point of origin. Time of receipt is STANDARD TIME at point of destination

0A091 (17)

0 CDU323 40 PD INTL=CD ROMA VIA RCA 30 1420=

LT AISSA WAYNE=

4750 LOUISE ST ENCINCO (CALIF)= 1957 MAR 30 AM 8 32

MY DARLING AISSA HAPPY BIRTHDAY STOP I HOPE YOU HAVE

MANY MANY MORE AND THAT I MAY HELP TO MAKE THEM HAPPY

STOP GIVE YOUR MOTHER A GREAT BIG KISS FOR ME=

:DAD:

THE COMPANY WILL APPRECIATE SUGGESTIONS FROM ITS PATRONS CONCERNING ITS SERVICE

*Even while shooting on location, John Wayne
kept in close contact with his family.*

This photograph of Aissa waterskiing in Acapulco
was framed on John's coffee table (1970).

The Waynes' Newport Beach home where John lived from 1966 until his death in 1979.

John, Marissa, and Pat Stacy (his personal secretary and close friend) in Alaska on board the Wild Goose *(1977).*

John Wayne's seven children in 1982. He lived to see twenty-one grandchildren before his death.

John Wayne's unmarked grave site in Newport Beach, California (1979).

outside with my family but felt the urge to dive back in. Flocks of deafening fans started shrieking and whistling the instant they spotted John Wayne. "DUKE, DUKE, DUKE, DUKE!" "I LOVE YOU DUKE." "HEY, DUKE, OVER HERE!" Safely inside the auditorium, Ethan and I were seated toward the back of the hall with our older brothers and sisters, while my parents were escorted to front center seats for the nominees and spouses. Looking around at the beautiful people milling inside, I recall feeling horribly embarrassed by my appearance. The Hollywood crowd all looked so exotically sexy. In dreadful contrast, I looked that night as if I were thirteen going on grandmother.

Oscar night was my first formal affair, and at first my mother said I could pick out my dress with my girlfriends. But my father overheard and overruled. "What do you mean you're going with your girlfriends? I can't believe this. I always thought I would be the one to go with you to pick out your first formal dress. I'm your father." *Precisely the point,* I thought. *You're the last person I want to go shopping for a dress with. I'm nearly fourteen. I'd like to go with my girlfriends.*

"All right daddy," I said.

I still could not stand up to him. I'd acquiesced. Again.

"You're dressing for an interview," my father always warned me before we met with the press, and both of us knew the translation: dress like Miss Goody Two Shoes. As Oscar night neared, I feared he'd make me purchase a dress I would never pick out myself, and of course my fear was confirmed. Its teal blue color was pretty, but its turtleneck collar, wrist-length sleeves and floor-length hem, all topped off by my hair, tightly balled up in a repressive bun, made me look boring and backwards and sober and terminally unhip. I should have been glad just to be there, but I was thirteen, and it was 1970. At that self-conscious point of my life, in that permissive era, on that auspicious evening, I still looked like daddy's little girl. At first, I felt so out of place I wished I was dead.

As all the acceptance speeches and music and glitz and

glamour got going, I became less self-involved. I was really at the Oscars! And I was sure my father was going to win. When I told him that before, over and over during the last several months, I wasn't sure if I meant it. Dustin Hoffman was pretty terrific in *Midnight Cowboy*. Still, though I'm not sure why, when Barbra Streisand sauntered to the podium to present the award for Best Actor, all my doubt dissolved. I recall thinking, Oh my God, this is perfect. Barbra Streisand, my heroine, anointing my father's crowning moment. Then she tore the envelope, withdrew the folded sheet, smiled, held it to her chest, and said, "I'm not going to tell you," and the thought occurred that I might have to run up and wring my heroine's neck.

"And the winner is . . . John Wayne for *True Grit.*"

Truth be told, my recollection of the rest of that dreamy moment is very slight. My memory of my father's final Oscar appearance, two months before his death, is really much more vivid. Still, I do recall Barbra Streisand saying the magic words, and me grabbing my brother Ethan so hard I startled him; desperately wishing I was sitting up with my mother and father so I could see the joy in their eyes; rising and cheering and laughing when my father said from up on the podium, speaking of his protracted standing ovation, "Wow, if I'd have known that, I'd have put on that eyepatch thirty-five years ago."

For all of us who loved my dad, it was a night of sublime satisfaction. There had never been any doubt of my father's bankability, but this validated his acting, and we all knew how much that secretly meant to him. Later that night, when I briefly saw my dad at our bungalow at the Beverly Hills Hotel, he was still floating on Oscar's rarified air.

"I love you, Daddy. I'm so happy for you."

I meant every word. My father just hugged me and beamed. Look at me, Aissa, his gleaming blue eyes seemed to be saying. Look at what they think of your old man.

23

In 1969, the Waynes were anything but immune to the confusing forces tearing apart American parents and children.

To complicate matters, that was the year I entered a public high school. By then, nearly all the children I knew had scratched the surface of self-sufficiency. They had been allowed to make their own errors, to see that to struggle or fail does not mean to be worthless, to form their own opinions, and to assume some responsibility for their own lives. As a catered-to Hollywood princess, entirely bypassing many of the normal, bruising-but-essential rites of growing up, I had no such street smarts. It didn't help that I was the youngest girl in my freshman class—having skipped lower fifth grade and started kindergarten early—and far younger than that in terms of maturity. Though I turned thirteen in 1969, I was as sheltered, naïve, and impressionable as if I were eight years old.

The population at Newport Harbor High, the oldest high school in town, was about ten times the size of my private elementary school, and countless times more lawless. Still perceiving me as his unprecocious angel, my father had no inkling what type of high school parties I went to. To this day Newport Beach is a cocktail-minded town, and there was reckless, mindless, damn-the-repercussions drinking among my classmates. While Newport adults were off skiing the Alps, Newport offspring flung open their parents' beveled glass doors to frenzied, keg-swilling rich kids who gleefully trashed the decors created by exorbitant interior designers. There were drugs at my new school, too. Newport Harbor High, if not exactly a center of social upheaval, did not go unstirred by the fumes of the '60s. Most of our football players smoked pot, as did our apple-cheeked cheerleaders. Our debutante girls popped diet pills as if they were M&Ms, and our honors students had visions on LSD. At Newport Harbor, like so many high schools back then, it was difficult discerning who belonged to what clique. Eventually, my mistake would be trying to be liked by all of them.

Although my corruption was still months off, the stage was set by my freshman troubles. By the time I'd graduated eighth grade, my schoolmates and I had at least become acquainted. With my imposing last name, I still felt apart, but I no longer felt like an alien. At Newport Harbor, the pointing, the whispering, the staring started anew. It had taken me three years to replenish my fickle self-confidence. In just several weeks of high school I lost much of it again.

Feeling totally lost in a large public school, for the first time in my life I earned poor grades. For all their strict ways, my private school teachers had deeply believed in the value of education. Some teachers at our public high school did too, but others all but admitted they saw themselves as underpaid baby-sitters. Unfamiliar with all this liberty, I became lazy, waiting for instruction that never came.

Stunned by my first set of tests, I was horrified by my grades. Whenever I brought home report cards in grade school, my father was stern, formal, inscrutable. A man whose drive to excel was nearly pathological, my dad expected straight A's and all my life I mostly made sure I received them. I knew my B's would be unsatisfactory, my C's grounds for angry chastisement. This time I'd gotten a couple of D's, and felt sure the man who could blow other actors off the screen would blow sky high at me.

To my amazement, my father was sympathetic. He said he understood how different private and public schools were, and that he was sure I would improve the next time. Then came the caveat: "You better," he threatened.

On top of my problems in class, I gained ten pounds by the end of my second semester. On my father's side of our family we all have my dad's legs, and mine grew even thicker as I discovered fast-food lunches of tacos and chips and burgers and fries. Ten pounds is a traumatic one-year weight gain for any girl of thirteen, and to me it felt disastrous. My mother, like many women back when I was a child, taught me that being a perfect women meant being beautifully thin.

I understand my mother's compulsion with looks. Women of her generation were more brainwashed than those of today; she also had no career, and she came to this country without much education. She was also married to John Wayne, who worked with scores of maturely beautiful women and lush ingenues. As a young girl, I never understood how my mother controlled her jealousies. I was only about four years old when my parents took me with them to a party thrown by the Foreign Press Association. All night long, a pretty, sad-eyed platinum blonde hung all over my father. I was more curious than resentful, until one of the woman's shoulder straps floated off her alabaster shoulder. Her bosom was exposed! Feeling this could not go unreported, I pulled my mother toward a corner. "Mom, you know that pretty blonde who's holding Dad's arm? She has no brassiere on!"

My mother glanced just for an instant. "That's Marilyn Monroe, honey," she said evenly. "She's always been very fond of your daddy."

My father never worked with Miss Monroe, but I would see his old love scenes on TV, or his new ones when we screened movies at home, and wonder how my mom felt about them. One time I asked her. "Mom, how can you stand to watch him in all those love scenes, with all those gorgeous women?"

"Your father is not a flirt," she said. "He makes me feel like I'm the only one."

My mother was right. By nature, my father was not flirtatious, and back then he certainly kept his focus on my mom. Still, I wonder now if she was entirely in touch with how she felt. I wonder if she believed the best revenge was looking good, so she buried her real feelings and overcompensated in some other way—as we Waynes were all so prone to. Looking back, I realize how much stress my mother placed on womanly beauty, how extremely conscious she was of her fetching appearance, and how disproportionate was the time she spent maintaining it. One wrinkle, one pound, one false eyelash out of place, and my mother ingested even less calories, played more tennis, and spent even more narcissistic hours a day her in front of her lighted mirror inside her private dressing room. Subsequently, her impressionable young daughter bought hard into a misguided notion: women and girls were only as valuable as their surface. "There is nothing more important than being beautiful," my mother told me.

Of course she was not alone in sending this message. I also received it from Madison Avenue, and to some extent from my dad. He always emphasized grades, and that I should be decent to others, and to give people second chances, and for all of that I am thankful. But he also told me not to voice my opinions, and only sporadically praised me for something I'd said or done, while frequently commending my appearance. "You're the prettiest girl in the world," he said in just those words, and when he did, he was not the same man who stood stiffly over my report cards, giving me only grudging respect for studying hard and bringing home A's. Times when I looked especially nice, my father seemed especially proud, loving, sanguine. I can see now how my values became distorted. My self-image was too closely bound with my looks, and too dependent on other people's approval. Like many young girls, I had set myself up, and been set up by others, to lose my self-esteem. And lose it I did, at times to the point of self-loathing, when I entered a high school in Newport glutted with beauties, gained ten pounds in one year, saw the disapproval in my mother's eyes, and the most important man in my life stopped telling me I was pretty.

It wasn't bad enough that so many girls at my Newport Beach high school were blond, thin, nubile, and tan. But my own mother emerged as a greater beauty in her forties than she'd ever been before. Her entire body hardened from ritual tennis, and her legs, already shapely, got even sexier with more definition. A more fully dimensional woman, but still relentless about staying trim, my mother made all too clear her dismay at her daughter's budding plumpness. "You're always eating lately. You've gained some weight, honey. I starve myself if I gain even one pound. All I eat is hard-boiled eggs—protein. I want you to read this diet book. You know that red outfit you want? I'll bet you'd look good in it. I'll buy it for you if you lose weight."

She didn't do it maliciously, but this didn't assuage the hurt. I *wanted* to be petite, wanted to look smashing in a tennis dress, wanted all the rewards of beauty. But it wasn't happening for me. I wasn't my mother and never would be. Meanwhile, my father had not yet mentioned my burgeoning weight; he no longer spoke at all about my appearance. All that superficial praise I'd received as a child, almost always for my looks, returned to haunt me in adolescence. I don't know how much I believe in epiphanies—I'm not sure life is that clear and well structured—but I distinctly remember my feelings the year I turned thirteen: *I am not pretty; I'm fat. I am not smart in school; I'm stupid. I am not fun to be with; I'm too self-conscious. I am none of the things I thought I once was, none of the things the adults in my life once told me I was. My life has been a lie.*

An oversensitive girl to begin with, my self-image plunged. During this time of cynicism and angst I was all raw nerves, reappraising not only myself, but nearly every dictum and every person, including my father. Surely all along he'd seen straight through my childhood "popularity." Surely he knew it was all about him, John Wayne, and I was just one means to ingratiation. If my father had lied about why people liked me, or if he had only misjudged things, perhaps he had lied or been wrong about others and other things too.

Perhaps smoking marijuana did not "lead to heroin."

Perhaps boys with long hair did not all look "ridiculous."

Perhaps every liberal wasn't "gutless," and perhaps the Vietnam War was not such a worthy thing.

Maybe, I told myself as the '60s boiled and screeched to their turbulent end, I had better start finding out for myself.

24

It was a mystery. At fourteen years old, I sensed that breaking away, examining life as unfiltered through John Wayne, was not just what I wanted but something I drastically needed. Why, then, did I feel so perplexed? I was a sophomore in high school, my father still had me literally sitting on his lap, and part of me still wanted to be there, content and protected. Other times when we were out in public, my father's smallest act could fill me with embarrassment, and I couldn't wait to escape him.

It was a mystery.

I suspect it was just as confusing for him. Like so many fathers, mine did not quite know how to emancipate his children, and did not entirely want to. That this was 1970 only roughened the waters. It was a radically shifting world, and even John Wayne could not deny it.

But he could certainly still run affairs inside his own home. Older than the rest of my girlfriends' fathers, he believed in old-fashioned strictures. While my girlfriends all ate dinner at six and could stay out weekend nights until one, I had to eat dinner at five and be home weekend nights by eleven, making me the group dullard who always had to leave everywhere first. I could not walk barefoot out of our house, not even to go to the beach, which was only two doors from our home. That all the kids at Bayshores went barefoot to the beach made no impact on him.

"*My* daughter doesn't walk barefoot," my father ordered. "*My* children wear shoes and socks."

It seems nitpicky now, but felt important back then to a young teenager, with my shoes and socks just one more glaring sign to the other kids that I didn't belong. The rare times I mustered the nerve to protest, my father yelled until I cried, then upbraided me for my tears.

"Why do you cry when I yell at you? What the hell are you crying for? Because you can't go out with bare feet? Jesus Christ."

I was crying about my life. But he couldn't see that and I couldn't say so. And moments later, when he was prepared for contrition, I had better be ready as well. Because he was directing every family scene, each familiar beat of it.

No proponent of youthful self-expression, he once ordered me back to my bedroom when I appeared with too much white makeup lining my eyelids.

"You look like a clown," he decided. "Get that goddamn stuff off your face or you're not leaving the house."

Today I look at old pictures and realize my father was right, I did look clownish beneath all that liner. But, again, at the time I felt steamrolled. In 1970 makeup ran to extremes. For once, I just wanted to blend in.

Too afraid of him to openly mount a rebellion, I did what teenagers do: I started sneaking around. First, I covertly bought a lavender bikini. I suppose I should have just asked him, but if John Wayne's daughter could not show her feet in public . . . besides, my father denounced them all—bikinis, hot pants, miniskirts—whenever he saw them on women in commercials. Sophomore year, a girlfriend lived on a house on the cliff and weekends we would go swimming and sunning in her backyard. At the end of the day, some of the other fathers picked up their daughters, still wearing their skimpy suits under their towels. But I'd leave our house in the morning wearing a one-piece, my bikini stuffed into my bag. Before returning home that night, I'd slip into my girlfriend's bedroom and back into my one-piece. It made me the butt of their jokes, but better that than the object of his rage.

I also became deceitful regarding my grades. Freshman year I'd been stunned when I'd faltered at school, but when it happened again the next year I felt disheartened. I told myself that I didn't care, and this was only partly untrue. Unlike so many teenagers, I was never consumed with anxiety over my future. If anything, I was too blasé. Why fret over the shape of things to come when my rich and famous father would always be holding my hand? The matter of grades was hardly resolved, though. My father was still into excellence, not excuses. I might be indifferent, but he would be irate. So I intercepted our mail and altered my D's to B's, puzzled but pleased that our teachers used pencils, then praying that my parents would never consult them. Somehow, no one ever found out.

Privacy also became an issue. Even when teenagers have some, they tell themselves and their friends they don't. I, in reality, had next to none. I didn't mind sharing a bedroom with my little sister, Marisa. There was too much silence and separation in our house already. But my father hated closed doors, and expressly forbade that his children's be shut unless we were dressing or taking showers. Unable to hide from him even inside my bedroom, I started fleeing our house at the slimmest opportunity. I regret much of this now, because it injured him, and perhaps because that's what I intended.

It wasn't rebellion, however, merely because rebellion was in the air (though that was attractive). For years, when my father went off to make a movie, I watched him pack up his bags, put on his Irish hat and walk out the door, then return a few months later feeling fulfilled, get rapidly crazed with boredom, and expect us to drop whatever we had going on and spin again in his orbit. In the past I'd done it, sometimes gladly, but now I was meeting boys, listening to rock and roll, cementing my friendships with girlfriends. I didn't want to go to Africa and Utah and Texas anymore. Ill-prepared to confront him, and not wanting him to know too much about my private life, I lied when he asked me to go on location, or spend a weekend with him on *The Wild Goose.* I always had bountiful excuses, but no substantial reasons, and my transparency pained my father even more.

"Oh, okay," he said, his giant voice now reduced. "You'd rather be at your friend's house than be with me. I'm home from making a movie and you'd rather be there. You don't care that I'm here, do you? You just don't care."

Hugging my father, reiterating my love, I felt such terrible . . . guilt?

Yes . . . and no. Mixed in with my guilt was the anger of all those repressive years. If still too cowed by him to show it, I was self-aware enough now to recognize that anger inside myself—and to recognize my father's manipulations. For the first time, my sole ambition in life was no longer to please him.

Still, I had no excuses and no recourse on my sixteenth birthday, when my father insisted I spend it with him on location in Durango. In his eyes, this was too major a milestone for me to beg out of. Knowing it, I didn't even try. Too bad my father and I could never really talk: I could have said this birthday was more precious to me than to him, being my Sweet Sixteen, and that getting marooned in beyond-forlorn Durango, without a single person my age, was the last way on earth I wanted to spend it. The film was *The Train Robbers.* The night of my party, my father brought out a cake and a few of the cast and crew sang happy birthday. He poured champagne all around, including a goblet for a reporter, and another goblet for me.

"Well, everybody," he said, "my daughter is sixteen years old. I guess it's about time she took her first sip of champagne."

Smiling as if I were having the time of my life, I lifted my glass as I might a foreign object, the picture of schoolgirl innocence.

In truth, I yearned for my own home and the camaraderie of my girlfriends. I'd also been drinking on weekends for nearly two years, and had long ago sampled champagne.

A few months later, *Good Housekeeping* ran a profile on my father, the family man and the Hollywood star, on location in Durango. My sixteen birthday, it said, was a blissful event for all.

The incendiary feelings did not come overnight. They had, in fact, been percolating for years, but now they seemed to possess me:

I don't want his fame. I don't want praise from adults whom I've never met—I haven't done anything—and I don't want contempt from people my age. I'm exhausted with constantly being prejudged, purely through the prism of my father. All my life it has always been, This is John Wayne's daughter. It has never been. This is Aissa.

I've had enough. I do not want to be John Wayne's daughter.

I was surprised to find the thought inside my brain, and yet each time I pushed it out it kept coming disturbingly back. For nearly my whole sophomore year, I played a bizarre game of denial, meeting new people and fabricating last names. I'd introduce myself as Aissa Brooks, Aissa Smith, Aissa Johnson, feigning confusion when I was scoffed at. "Aissa *Wayne*? Me, John Wayne's daughter? Sorry. You've got me mixed up with some other girl."

Of course my ruse rarely worked. Other girls could escape their parents by traipsing out their front door, but I could never outdistance John Wayne. Definitely not in Newport Beach, where I felt his palpable presence wherever I went, but nowhere more than at school.

———

"You must be a right-wing nut," I was flatly told several times by older boys with long hair. "You must be for the war. You're John Wayne's daughter."

I was also a teenager. Having other kids my age call me "right wing" left me speechless and made me sick. Not yet fifteen, too turned off by politics to firmly grasp the complicated tempest of Vietnam, I was old enough to know that reactionaries were out, and that this rendered my dad—and myself by association—so far out as to be obsolete. I didn't know how common, how nearly predetermined it is, for children to feel embarrassment toward their parents, whether their parents advocate bigger wars or saving the dolphins. I never considered my long-haired accusers' home lives, never stopped to think that perhaps when they saw their parents smoking pot, or heard them chanting "Make Love, Not War," they felt the same twinge I did when my father prattled on about "Commies," or plastered another bumper sticker— "The Marines are looking for a few good men"—on the fender of his green Pontiac station wagon. Lacking this perspective, certain I must be a rotten person and daughter, I confided my feelings in no one. I did not even tell Debbie, and yet there it was again, my dark deep secret; I was embarrassed to be my father's daughter.

As if to magnify my dilemma, to illustrate the gap between myself and the rest of my generation, the Hollywood press came along. First a fan magazine sent a crew out to our house to photograph the John Waynes—"Aissa, you're dressing for an interview"—and that day we all went through our paces. That my parents no longer shared a bedroom, that I was walking around Newport Beach denying my last name was Wayne, that my father had started slapping my brother Ethan from time to time, did not so much as peek through our sunny veneer. This was our form of work, what Hollywood families did. We were old hands at "being on" for the press.

The instant the photo session ended, I peeled off my knee-length skirt, my fluffy white sweater and cordovan loafers, and forgot about it. When I saw the printed issue several

weeks later, it was Oscar night all over again. On the opposite page from our photos the magazine ran a spread on the
Elizabeth Taylors. Not only her children, but Liz herself,
were all tie-dyed and punked out, while we Waynes seemed
mired in the Eisenhower America. The fanzine people, of
course, had not said we'd be juxtaposed with Liz and her
kids, and I'm sure to many readers the dichotomy was amusing. Even I find it funny, today. Then, it was not exactly the
way I envisioned myself appearing in the national press.

But that was only my vanity. By my sophomore year, my
doubts about my father's conservatism, his high-profile pro-
Vietnam stance, had started cutting more deeply. First, when
I'd be with my girlfriends and they'd point to older Newport
boys I'd never met and say, "That guy just got drafted," I'd
respond with interest, but interest tempered by distance. I
didn't know them, and I didn't know if they'd ever actually
go to war. Then a boy named Rick, a friend of Debbie's older
brother, received his notice. Having a bit of a secret crush on
him, I became nervous at the notion of Rick's fighting. It
started me thinking new thoughts, and one day it hit me: "My
brother. What about my brother?" Ethan was only nine. His
going to Vietnam was a long shot. But if what the commenta-
tors kept saying was true, this war started back at the end of
the 1950s, and was still looking brutally endless in 1970, then
Ethan *could* go, and then what might befall him? At fifteen,
I was adept at telling lies, but the answer I gave myself carried with it the chill of truth: my little brother could die.

This was emotional, not political, and on a purely emotional level I started disliking the Vietnam War. It was a
serious breakthrough for me, not because I was right and my
father was wrong, but because I made up my mind on my
own about something important. But I never told him, not
then, not even after we pulled out our troops. When it came
to the most divisive war in American history, my father had
little patience for either debate or dissent. He was remark-
ably well read on foreign affairs, and had rubbed shoulders
with generals; his knowledge alone was enough to intimi-
date me. Besides, he was John Wayne, and I wasn't up to that

challenge. I still recalled, too, what my father had told me throughout my childhood, and was still telling me in high school: "Don't voice your opinion too much, and you won't sound like a fool."

Since father knew best, I heeded his words. At home I ate, slept, bathed, and muffled my feelings. Away from my father I lived out my double life.

25

From doctoring my grades, I graduated to taking diet pills my second year in high school.

Having inherited my mother's compulsion to stay thin, I believed the ten pounds I'd gained in a year looked more like thirty. One day, sitting in ceramics class, two pretty and popular girls slid out a baggie of pills, a menagerie of reds, yellows, whites, and purples. I didn't know the girls well, but I knew they were cheerleaders and belonged to a social group known as the "soshes." I wanted them to befriend me, but more than that I wanted my body to look like theirs.

"Try these, you'll lose weight for sure," one of the soshes said, in a voice sounding stuck on fast forward. I think she was already on one that morning. I took a handful of Dexedrine and dropped them into my purse. For one week of mornings prior to school, I locked our bathroom door and gulped my amphetamines. I lost a few pounds, but I also acquired teeth clenched so tight my jaw ached, and concentration so scattered my train of thought never left the station. That weekend I flushed the remaining dexies.

Around this time, my father announced a new rule: every afternoon at five our family would gather for dinner. His intent was for us to be close, to try and subvert the forces pulling us apart, but no one wanted to be there other than he. Ethan and I had to run in off the beach to eat, one full hour before the rest of our friends. Even my mother seemed resentful; their marriage was failing and she had other places she'd rather be. Dinners were often the tensest part of our day. Although my father worked hard at controlling his temper, he could not quell his urge to dictate. Asking about our lives, he'd allow us to answer, but then he'd wind up issuing lectures. The worst nights, my father rode Ethan throughout our meal. Though my father never hit me, never even spanked me, he had no such qualms about his boy. He never struck Ethan at dinner, but my father's furious looks carried with them the musk of violence.

Once on our boat, my father asked Ethan if he'd just told a lie, and Ethan looked up and said "Yes." When Marisa or I lied about something small, and then confessed, my father always said, "Well, I'm glad you didn't lie twice—just don't lie to me again." But then, on the boat, because it was Ethan, my father smashed his face with the hard bony back of his heavy hand. The only other time I recall him hitting Ethan with real force, my father slapped him so hard that the kid flew across the room. I wanted to shout, cry out, demand that my father stop. But I dared not intervene. Not when he was like this.

My father called Ethan "Big Stuff," mostly with pride but sometimes with sarcasm. Even when Ethan was very young, he was not allowed to cry. Once, while my father sat playing bridge with three of his friends, I pushed open the kitchen door just as Ethan was rushing in sipping a Coke. The swinging door propelled the glass bottle into my brother's mouth. My father didn't see it, only saw his son crying, and hollered at Ethan in front of all the adults.

"Go to your room and stay there!" he ordered. "Don't you open your mouth! I don't want to hear any crying out of you!"

I meekly followed Ethan into his bedroom, where he sat alone on the edge of his bed, his front tooth knocked crooked, blood dripping down his chin from the wound in his gums. Rushing back to the card game, I told my father Ethan was really cut, his mouth was bleeding badly. The eyes of his friends were fixed on their cards. His own eyes clouded with bottomless guilt, my father excused himself and hurried to Ethan's room.

"Oh, God, Ethan," my father said when he saw his child's blood. "I'm so sorry for being so hard on you. I just don't want you to cry."

The years passed and Ethan grew up, but not quickly enough for my dad. The more his own health deteriorated, the more swiftly he saw his own life nearing its end, the faster he rushed Ethan through his childhood. But how does a boy prepare to become the man of the house when the man of the house is John Wayne? There was no room, and besides, my brother was just a boy, unprepared for that type of responsibility. Helplessly, I watched them grow further apart. On the sets of films, I could see that Ethan was drawn not to my dad, but always to the younger, rowdier, more energetic stunt men. Ethan went to them to whip around a football, to watch them ride their motorcycles—it ate my father up.

But it wasn't only Hollywood stunt men: my father became enraged at the thought of his children growing close to any older man except himself. His dearest friend at the time was a man named Chick Iverson. In his middle forties, Chick owned a sports-car dealership in Newport, and was fast friends with John Derek. John and his wife, Linda Evans, were still on friendly terms with Ursula Andress, John's ex, and the glamorous trio appeared at several of Chick Iverson's parties. A child of Hollywood, raised to admire physical beauty, I was struck by their sheer perfection, especially Ursula's and John's. By virtue of his dazzling friends alone, I decided Chick Iverson must be an exceptional person.

My junior year, I'd just started dating Chick Jr., Chick Iverson's seventeen-year-old son. One rainy Newport weekend I cancelled our date, feeling fluish and weak. Later that night while driving home, Chick's car skidded down a rain-slick ravine. Chick Jr. died three days later.

His father could not bear it. He and his son had been extremely close, and now his boy was gone. Although we could never replace him, from the day Chick Jr. died, I think his father saw Ethan and me as his surrogate teenage children. Helping him cope with his loss, I learned that for all his slick sophistication, Chick was also a very intelligent man. He was older, he knew things, and yet he listened. I found I could talk to Chick about almost anything, even boys. At his invitation, my brother and I went to see Chick about three times a week at his office.

One day my father found out.

Please understand, my father loved Chick Iverson. Their greatest bond was a passion for the sea, and that each could make the other man laugh. After the car wreck, while Chick Jr. lay in his coma, my father went to the hospital and held Chick Sr. in his arms.

Now, he was infuriated at Ethan and me.

"You go to my best friend when you have a problem? You don't come and talk to me? *He's* not your father. *I'm* your father."

"Dad," I said, trying somehow to downplay. "Mr. Iverson's just a good friend, like an uncle. We go to the car lot. The sports cars are neat."

"He's not your father!"

The friendship between my father and Chick survived. But within it, after this, ran currents of loss and pain. Ethan and I promised my dad that next time we'd turn to him. Seeing how badly we hurt him, at the time I think we both meant it. But we were still the same children, he the same father, and "next time" turned out to be empty words.

*

Sophomore and junior year I felt pressure jut in from both sides. Pressure from people my age to party, pressure from my father not to publicly shame him. Though he still looked at me and saw innocence, drugs was too blaring an issue for him to simply pretend his teenage daughter would never confront them. Newport Beach had money, and its children the wherewithal to buy drugs.

Although he danced around the word *drugs,* my father was plain on potential repercussions. "I worked fifty years for my reputation," he warned me. "I worked damn hard. If you get caught doing something wrong, or if you're with other *kids* who are doing things wrong, it will go right in the papers. You'll ruin fifty years of my hard work. You'll ruin my name. So really think about it, before you do anything stupid."

I did think about his reputation, not enough to stop me, but enough for my pot-smoking peers to brand me as paranoid. Each time I bolted up at the smallest sound, they told me, "You're just paranoid. And the only reason you can't smoke pot without getting paranoid is that you don't have a strong personality." In ways they were right, but not for the reasons they thought. Had I been a stronger person, I'd have never smoked pot in the first place. My father's warnings aside, I never liked pot's effects. I felt groggy and lethargic, and I thought the other kids were laughing at me. Still, I smoked anyway. It wasn't enough for me to be liked by some of my peers—everyone had to accept me. I was exactly the opposite of the typical young kid who runs around smoking and drinking and getting in trouble to try and grab some attention. I had too much attention, too many stares from too many eyes. All I sought now was to be seen as the girl next door, and this was the early '70s. The girl next door was smoking marijuana, perhaps dropping LSD.

Too scared of LSD to even experiment, in countless other respects I mimicked my peers. Though my father gave me and my mother charge cards from several exclusive dress shops, I completely stopped using them. When girls and guys at parties downed beer from their bottles, I drank beer from

mine; only a spoiled Hollywood bitch would request a glass.
I conformed and conformed and conformed, and I even "got
high"—despite secretly hating the feeling, despite secretly
feeling panicked. I could never confess this uncoolness, so
instead I'd accept the joint, take a deep, defiant drag—who's
a priss now?—meanwhile praying the cops would not smash
down the door, followed by reporters, followed by fire-and-
brimstone headlines besmirching our family name, followed
by . . . my father.

My father!

"You're just paranoid," one of the other girls said. I was
in the midst of a pot-smoking party, and I'd just heard a
sudden noise outside the bedroom. There were seven or eight
of us, teenage girls, in a smoke-filled beachfront bedroom,
coughing on joints rolled in red-white-and-blue papers
resembling American flags.

"I heard the garage door!" I said.

"You're just paranoid."

"No, I'm telling you—"

My girlfriend's mother burst in.

"What are you doing?" she asked, her nose pointed up
and sniffing the smoky air. She was young, and newly single.

"Smoking cigarettes."

Cigarettes didn't come papered in red, white, and blue,
and I knew she would tell all our parents.

The only way to save myself, the only conceivable way
to circumvent my father, was deviously. In a few subtle
places I unhooked and unplugged our telephones. Though I
still don't understand how, for one night and a day my
scheme went undetected, but the very afternoon our phones
went back on their hooks and into their walls, my girlfriend's
mother rang through.

I came in from school and my father said, "We need to
talk." Petrified, bracing, I skulked behind him into the
kitchen. "Aissa," he said without raising his voice. "I love
you very much. The people that give you that stuff, they don't
love you the way that I do. You can take their word that this

stuff is good, or you can listen to me when I tell you it's bad. The stuff is bad, Aissa. Now whose word are you going to take, someone who's known you and loved you all your life, or someone you met two days ago?"

Actually, I thought, *I've known most of the girls for years.*

"Are you listening, Aissa? Whose word are you going to take?"

"Your's, Dad. I'm sorry. I'll never do it again."

My father had called me no names. Had not used rage or self-righteousness. Had not invoked his public image, his fifty years of hard work.

He must have a motive.

Yet he seemed sincere.

For the next several days I toyed with a farfetched notion: perhaps he isn't the enemy.

One night about three months later, in the shag-carpeted back of an older boy's van, I sat drinking beer from a can with a few of his friends and two of my girlfriends. Sure, it was after curfew, but we thought we played it safe by parking the van on a dark, drowsy side street and shutting all the curtains. First came a beam of refracted light, then a sharp rap on metal.

"Everyone out!" a male voice shouted outside.

We scurried outside the van to the sight of flashlight-wielding policemen. For ninety minutes, the two uniformed patrolmen stripped apart the boy's van, presumably searching for drugs. We'd only been drinking beer, the officers found no drugs. They led us back to their car and drove us down to the station.

The police saw my last name, but did not seem to know I was John Wayne's daughter, and I didn't volunteer the information. There were no mug shots, no fingerprints, no clanging cell doors, no Good Cop/Bad Cop scene out of a movie. The police didn't even charge us. But they did detain us long into the night, long enough for us to contemplate ourselves and our glum surroundings. One officer took the boys into one room, while my girlfriends and I sat blinking at the gun-metal gray walls of another.

What am I doing here? Next time, there really may be drugs, and maybe I'll find out how it feels to spend time caged up behind bars. Why am I using drugs anyway? I'm not jittery and mixed up enough when I'm straight? And that's what I am—I'm straight. I am straight, and I don't want to screw up my life, and no amount of pot or un-touched charge cards or fraying jeans will ever change the person I am at heart. So who am I trying to seem?

My breath was getting short and something tight and oppressive fluttered inside my chest. I thought I might hyperventilate.

By the time the police called everyone's parents, my mother, I knew, would be sitting home terrorized, all her fears that some Hollywood-stalking crazy had kidnapped or hurt me triggered again by the shrill late-night ring of the phone. My dad, thank God, was out of town on business.

Since there'd been no arrest reports made, the press never found out I'd been taken in. Neither did my father. As we drove home from the station at three A.M., my tired and livid mother was not in the mood to talk. She said we'd discuss this in the morning, and that she would not tell my father, not *this* time, and there better not be a next time. As my mother drove home in the darkness I noticed my hands were quivering.

26

The summer before my junior year, on the Southwestern set of *The Undefeated,* I stood on the side with my dad watching Rock Hudson perform a scene.

"Look at that face," my father said admiringly, without turning to look at me. "What a waste of a face on a queer. You know what I coulda done with that face?"

I was staggered, for two reasons. First, that Rock Hudson, who I thought gorgeous, was homosexual. Back then, it never occurred to me that a good-looking man could be gay. Secondly, that my father had spoken to me, his daughter, in a manner he always reserved for men. Crude or not, this was Boy Talk, a party I'd never been privy to. Since my father did not seem to want any reply, I merely stood there, dumbfounded and mute.

That was about as close as we ever came to discussing sex. Not surprisingly back then, both my parents found it difficult to talk about sexual behavior with their children. My mother was very good at explaining my period, but that was as far as she went, and since my high school had no sex education, I learned the facts of life from other young girls. This naturally led to distortions.

When I was twelve, a girl three years older spent the weekend with her parents on our boat. One night as we curled up in our sleeping bags, the Turtles' "Hello, I Love You" came over the radio. My sage older friend turned up the music so no one could eavesdrop, and began explaining to me the mechanics of sex, what part of the husband's anatomy went where on the wife. But what she said and what I perceived were not at all the same thing. I thought she said the man peed inside the woman, and that's how people made babies.

"What?" I said. "That's awful. It's the grossest thing I've ever heard."

"I knew it," she replied. "You're too young, I never should have told you. Promise me you won't tell your parents."

I gave her my word, and for one year I went nowhere with my confusion. When I turned thirteen, my understanding of sex was still sketchy at best, but that year I got my first real kiss. Only a freshman, I somehow revealed my crush to the sophomore boy who'd been stirring all these new feelings inside me all year. By then my girlfriends and I had read parts of that book—*Everything You Always Wanted to Know About Sex But Were Afraid to Ask*—but it all became a blur when my lips met the sophomore boy's on the dance floor. I was in love and felt that we should get married.

By the end of the following school week, the boy's critique got back to me. He told all his friends I was a terrible kisser, the worst he'd ever met.

I was humiliated to tears, and after this I had even more than the normal teenage girl's fear of discovering sex: fear of kissing badly, fear of being called slut, fear of pregnancy, fear of boys getting fresh not because they liked me, or even because they thought I was pretty, but so they could run lying and boasting to other boys that they just had their way with John Wayne's daughter. I was so embarrassed by my sexuality, I even felt timid the first week I wore my training bra, certain my father would notice and disapprove. I was intensely relieved when he didn't.

My fear of sex was reinforced by all the talk around our house about the new eroticism in Hollywood movies: that it was "repulsive" and "bad." To back up his code of sexual beliefs, my dad did not allow me to date until my senior year. Even then he seemed uncomfortable, tossing out mild but skeptical comments about my potential suitors, especially those with long hair. One day some young local Marines awarded my father a plaque at our house. When they left my dad told me, "That's the kind of boy I can see you with, Aissa." They seemed like nice boys, but they all had crew cuts, and I didn't care for the look. My supreme fear my senior year was that some long-haired boy I really liked would come to pick me up and my law-laying father would grill and bombard him. So even after my father said I could date, I usually lied, meeting the boys in town and telling my dad I was out for a night with my girlfriends.

One night I will never forget, my father nearly shot a boy I knew. Around ten P.M., I drove home from Pat Kelly's, my first real boyfriend, with Pat's roommate, Rick. My father collected 16 millimeter versions of his old movies, and we wanted to watch one on Rick's and Pat's projector. Thinking it was late and my father was sound asleep, I took Rick straight through our garage to the room behind our bookcase, where my father stored his reels. My dad must have heard us and feared that he had intruders. For what he called "security reasons," he always kept several guns stashed around our house. Reaching inside his nightstand for his revolver, my father stole back to the bookcase.

"Aissa?" he yelled.

Not knowing my father was holding a gun, I didn't reply.

He had this rule about people taking his movies without his permission.

"Aissa," he yelled again.

My father also had a monumental pet peeve: he went berzerk when his children did not respond the instant he called out their name.

"Answer him!" Rick whispered. "Answer him!

Too late. Pushing through the door, my father stuck his cocked gun in Rick's face.

"Look at this!" he screamed at Rick. "Do you see this gun? I almost blew your goddamn head off!" Rick shook and shivered and couldn't speak.

Trembling with outrage, my father started on me. "Don't you *ever* come into this house without coming straight to my room and telling me you're here!"

"But I thought you were asleep!"

"I don't give a damn! I almost shot his head off!"

After that ghastly night I practically shouted whenever I walked in the door. Rick never came back to the Wayne's.

I fell for Patrick Kelly at my senior prom. Tall and solidly built, at twenty years old Patrick was an official "older guy." He was also another girl's date that night. I'd come to prom with Johnny, a friend living at Bayshores, but Johnny had one critical failing: he wasn't Patrick Kelly. It was tradition after Newport Harbor's Senior Prom to stay out all night and bounce from party to party. Through some monumental miscommunication, I believed my father said I could sleep that night at a girlfriend's.

Patrick Kelly was having a party and said I could bring along Johnny, and Johnny at first was happy to go. But the more time I spent around Patrick, Johnny kept suggesting we check out some other parties. I finally told Johnny to take my car and pick me up later.

That was my first mistake. Rather than buy me a car that March when I turned sixteen—customary parental behavior in Newport Beach—my father had waited nine months, until Christmas 1972. That December morning he gave me two modest presents. I tried seeming grateful but actually felt slighted, since this was so unlike him. Around five that afternoon he handed me a cigar box containing a pair of keys. With no emotion, he told me follow him out to our garage. Parked there was a glistening new yellow Porsche 914! After crying with happiness, I thought about what my less-privileged classmates might say. For a girl intent on fitting in, the sports car did not follow the plan. But who cared? I was human. After all those years of driving around in my father's green station wagon, I fell in love with my sleek new wheels.

My Porsche still smelled new the night I gave it to Johnny to take to the other party. By the time the sun rose on Patrick's rented beach house, our group had drained many beers, blasted the Rolling Stones, and already returned from a bleary-eyed five A.M. breakfast. I was hungover and exhausted, but oh, was I happy. Patrick and I hadn't kissed, but I told him I'd liked him for months, and Patrick said he liked me too, he just hadn't known how to say so.

Patrick had a message on his machine, left there by Johnny while we'd been out eating breakfast. Johnny said he wrecked my Porsche. It wasn't *driveable,* so he left it there on the side of the road. I was terrified, *terrified* at the fit I knew my father would throw.

"I have to get home," I said to Patrick. "My father is going to kill me."

The sun that June morning was already hot. When Patrick climbed hastily into his car without his shirt on, I gave it no thought, my mind locked on the rampage I knew I was heading into. As we turned into my complex the full implication came over me: I am not in my own car, I'm not with my original date, and the boy I'm with has no shirt on.

"That can't be my father!" I said.

It could. It was. As I later found out, my father stayed up all night in his silk pajamas, knocking on doors of gossipy neighbors and angrily pacing our driveway, because *he* thought I'd be home by two A.M.

Now he was still in his pajamas, and nearly out to the street. Restraining his self and his temper, my father spoke in a tightly clipped voice. "We've been looking for you all night. Get in the house."

Knowing better than even to glance at Patrick Kelly, I said "bye" over my shoulder and hurried past my dad with eyes trained straight ahead. I waited, and waited, and waited, but my father never came into my room. For the next twenty-four hours he was cold and distant, barely speaking my name. When he finally came to my bedroom I told my father the story without any lies.

"If I gave you what you deserved," my father said, "I'd have to ground you forever. So let's just forget it." Except for growling once about the repair bill, my father never mentioned it again.

That story shows my dad in all his formidable unpredictability. Like the time I was caught smoking pot, I was sure I'd be crucified for the Porsche, and each time my father took no punitive action. Each instance, the relief I felt was only surpassed by my shock and confusion. Today, I'm sure my father suppressed his rage for fear of driving his teenager daughter further away. Today, I can see that it all made textbook Wayne family sense. When the Wayne children did nothing wrong, that's often when we were yelled at, and when we deserved real reproof we got off the hook. No wonder we were all such nervous kids. For children, erratic fathers are scary.

How funny people can be. Because for all of my father's flaws, for many years I was drawn to boys and men in his image. Boys and men with big voices, big bodies, big gestures, boys and men who wanted to make all my choices and regulate my life. That's how I related to males, because that's the way I related to my dad. When I realized this unflattering truth about myself, at first I was deeply ashamed. Since I thought no other father on earth could influence another woman the way my father did me, I believed that I was uniquely, emotionally, defective. I eventually learned that many, many other women have similar feelings about their fathers. Even today, I am still not entirely free of my father's control. But I know I'm not alone.

27

By the end of 1973—the year my parents split up—my main emotion was relief. Seventeen, I'd long given up the fantasy of the perfect home life. Their marriage, in fact, was a wreck, and at least for the moment beyond working out. Though they rarely fought, the tension between them was making everyone skittish.

Thanksgiving was near, and my father and I had still not discussed his problems with my mom. In addition, I had still never seen him cry about the prospect of losing my mother. Like so many American men of his generation, my father believed if a man was to call himself a man, he must wear a kind of armor, male and indestructible, that concealed his fears and deepest feelings from his family. Particularly to

John Wayne, showing fear and pain was for women and children.

With time and circumstance people can change, even patriarchal fathers born in 1907. And something changed that winter between my father and me. One night after an awful fight with my mother, he entered my bedroom and sat on my sister's bed. Marisa was not around, or he never would have come in there. As my father sat down I could see tears inching down his stubbled face. When first he saw me looking he turned away. Then with the side of one thick finger, my father wiped his cheeks, turning his wet and unashamed eyes back to me.

"Honey," he said, "your mother and I are having some serious problems. I love her so much, I love you, I love our family, but I have to work—you know I have to—to support us, and I know it's hard on your mother. She doesn't understand . . ."

His upper body rocking, his words spilling out between too many extra breaths, my father stopped speaking and started to cry. Once his tears unloosed, they came and they came. Tears. No sobbing or other sounds. Only tears. With no consideration of my actions, no thought of our future or past, I crossed to Marisa's bed and I held him. He made no effort to stop me and we sat on my sister's bed for several trembling moments, nothing withheld, my father and I as one, frozen in the sorrow and the still. I was seventeen. My father was sixty-six. We had crawled to this naked communion, this beautiful frightening point of no return, and why it had taken so long never entered my mind. Pulling him close, I knew we would never again be quite the same two people.

Now everything's out in the open. Our lives are more honest now. I silently told myself that through the winter and spring, and at first our new arrangement suited me. After my mother moved out that December—by mutual accord, while my father was out of town—she and my dad were more friendly than when they had shared a home. Custody wasn't an issue since neither sought a divorce. They lived five miles apart, no distance at all in Southern California, my dad in the house at Bayshores, my mom at our Big Canyon condo. I kept clothes and belongings with both and made sure my shuttles between them were even. But I selfishly preferred to stay with my mom. She was more lenient, and I was seventeen.

For me it was all fairly convenient and far less stressful, but as time passed, I started seeing that "honest lives" can hurt too. My parent's civil smiles when the family was all together would vanish the moment the other one left. I know they tried not to, but their bitterness often seeped out. My mother complained that he was irritable and stubborn about working and that she could not spend entire summers up in Alaska on our boat. Whenever I'd visit my dad he always spoke of other things first, then brought the conversation to her. "A woman should stay with her husband. Your mother gets mad because I have to work. Where the hell does she think we get our money?"

I hurt for them both and tried staying neutral, gently taking the side of whomever I was with. But I found myself feeling more pain for my father. My mother opened a restaurant, the Fernleaf Cafe, and was busy with that, while my dad was growing older, more tired, still working as hard but not nearly as often. I'd never seen him so torn up, nor so lonely. I was used to him needing our feeding; he always needed that. But I wasn't prepared to see his self-pity. If I missed a few days of visits, he charged that I didn't love him. "I know you don't love me, Aissa. If you loved me you'd spend more time here."

As it did the night he cried in my arms, seeing my father like this filled me with more emotions than I was equipped to sort out. My mother was gone, he needed me now, and I wanted it. Still, I felt so awkward. My father talked about he and my mom, my turn came to speak, and all I could muster was something like "Dad, I know she still loves you," or, "Dad, you should really try talking things out." His disappointed eyes told me he wanted more, and sometimes that angered me. After all those years of treating me like his baby girl—smile sweetly and don't have any opinions—he wanted to snap his fingers and have me turn into a woman.

Several months after my mother moved out, the more upset I saw her becoming, the more certain I felt she and my father would reunite. I think she realized her work, her new friends, her religion, her tennis, all gave her something worthwhile, but also that she still deeply loved her husband. One day she wrote him a long letter, and shortly after that they met at the Fernleaf Cafe. My mom never showed the letter to me and I never felt I should ask, but I was sure she'd return home and say she was moving back in. Instead she came back to the condo crying.

Without telling my mother, I jumped in my car and sped to the house on Bayshores, having no idea what I might say. My father sat outside on a lounge chair, an umbrella giving him shade. Sitting erect, he still looked sad, but no longer self-pitying. When I asked what happened, he spoke as he sometimes did about giving people chances.

"You give someone a chance," he said, "and then you give them a second chance. But after two chances that's it. After that you start to lose your dignity, and that's where you have to draw the line."

I didn't know what he meant, didn't know what had transpired the past days, weeks, months, years, between him and my mother. But I understood my father's tone and the language of his body. I felt my own muscles go flaccid, and suddenly feeling sleepy I went inside to lie down. For now, the marriage was through.

28

It was a tangled evolution, coming in fits and starts. But my father was learning to let go.

The first breakthrough came when I graduated high school. By my junior year, I had quit smoking pot completely. It was fairly easy to do since I'd never enjoyed its effects in the first place, and having been scared to death by those two policemen tearing apart the older's boy van—looking for drugs—the night I spent several hours in jail. I still knew plenty of kids who did drugs, but I stopped hanging around them, and became more involved with my school work. By my junior year I had done some maturing, and upon my graduation, my father, reassured by my grades my last two years, made no strident fuss when I said I wanted to work for a year before enrolling at USC. That March I turned eighteen and he allowed me to spend my birthday at home, in Newport, with friends, even though he was off on location. "You're no longer a baby," said the note my father sent from Seattle with a pungent bouquet of flowers. "You've flown the coop. Love, Dad."

I decided to test his words that summer. He asked me to fly to London, where he was filming *Brannigan,* and I said I would love to, but first could I see parts of Europe, with Patrick Kelly, Debbie, and her boyfriend? The first surprise came when my father said yes; the next when the four of us joined him in London, and he didn't say an embarrassing word about our sleeping arrangements the past two weeks. In London he did put up the boys in separate hotels, but then he picked up their tab, which the guys had planned on paying. It meant a great deal to me, unsure as I was about his feelings toward Patrick Kelly. An older boy, with long hair, Patrick never went out of his way to endear himself to my dad, remaining courteous but cool. But throughout our stay my father was warm and relaxed and gracious. Just who was doing the growing up here?

During this time my mother arrived in London, in what I presumed to be a final attempt to reconstruct their marriage. The week before leaving Newport, she'd telephoned London seeking my father and been told he was spending the weekend in Ireland—with Pat Stacy, his secretary. My mom was in London for only a couple days before she and my father fought. My mother left in a rage, certain her husband had started romancing his thirty-two-year-old secretary.

I don't know if that was true, but I never saw Pat Stacy as any threat to the possibility of my parents reconciling. Born in Louisiana, Pat was a spiky-haired brunette with dark brown eyes and a cute petite figure. She'd been hired by my father's secretary, Mary St. John, to be groomed as Mary's successor when she retired. I liked Pat. Though at first I saw she was starstruck by my dad—everyone saw, since Pat made it impossible not to—I sensed as time went on that she honestly cared for him. While he was alive, I never felt Pat was out to exploit my dad.

About four years after he died I had second thoughts. Pat then had the gumption to write a book about herself and my father, glamorizing, romanticizing, hyperbolizing their "love affair." Among other fanciful things, Pat said my father made no secret of his affection for her in front of myself and the other children. In truth, he was standoffish toward Pat when I was around. When they were alone, I'm sure he felt grateful for her company. With him and my mother estranged, she was a feminine soul when he needed one. And although my father groused when the tabloids got wind of their "romance," blaming Pat for talking too much and too freely, he probably enjoyed it. An aging Hollywood star with a younger woman—it was good for his image. Despite his physical problems at that stage of his life, perhaps my father and Pat even made love on occasion.

But was he in love with Pat Stacy? And did they have the gushy romance Pat depicted in her book?

I don't think so. Had my father felt about Pat the way she described, I think he would have married her. As Michael Wayne used to say, "John Wayne is the marrying kind," and that was true: whether with Josephine, or Chata, or my mother, my dad was never loathe to admit when he was in love, and never shy about either divorce or marriage. Yet he never married Pat, even though my mother offered him a divorce. He never invited Pat to move in with him. Instead, to her annoyance, even after he moved her office into the house on Bayshores, where Pat did secretarial work by day, my father still rented a separate house for Pat to live in. That wasn't his style when he was in love.

Had Pat not written that book, I'd have never mentioned any of this, but the book seemed so far removed from the truth I felt that I should.

My freshman year at USC I shared off-campus housing with Debbie, but neither one of us was equipped to live on our own. Our small apartment was littered with filthy dishes and soiled clothes. Rather than simply cleaning up, Debbie and I took out our bad moods on each other. In the first significant crisis of our friendship, I responded typically: instead of discussing it, addressing the real problem—our parents had spoiled us rotten when we were kids—I ate every night to dull my depression.

One weekend at Bayshores, my father noted my weight gain. He called me "fat" in front of his card-playing cronies, but he didn't stop there. "You're so fat!" he went on, with what sounded to me like glee. "Aissa, you've gotta do something about it! Look how you fat you are! How could you do that to yourself?"

Was this his idea of motivation?

They hadn't been drinking; he couldn't blame that.

Was he waiting for me to cry?

I rushed from the room silently cursing him. Hating him. I hated him for the rest of that day, refusing to answer my phone despite knowing who it was. What could his words do? They couldn't change the humiliation I felt. They couldn't change the past.

When I finally picked up the phone, I went right to it.

"Dad. You cannot talk to me like that. You made a fool out of me in front of all your friends. How could you do that to me?"

He was apologetic, giving me all that ancient crap about how much he loved me, how much I mattered. Please, could I just forgive him?

Forgive him? To break the chain, to get him to see past himself and look at who you were, you *couldn't* forgive him. Why had it taken me so long to understand that?

"Dad!" I cut him off, surprising myself. "Don't ever talk like that to me. I'm serious."

"I won't," my father said, after a long pregnant pause. "I swear it, Aissa, I won't."

It was a start.

Back in the sixties my father was churning out hits, every studio sought him, and his family's spending was a minor concern. But by the mid-seventies, money for my father approached an obsession. Like many Depression-shaped children made good, in his wallet he still carried thick wads of big bills. He still owned a home and a condominium, lucrative livestock and ranch land in southern Arizona, and had part ownership of several other financial interests. Still, this seemingly gave him no peace. Increasingly he fretted over the IRS, the huge expense of owning a boat, his exorbitant medical insurance, his ebbing cash flow, how severely he'd been mismanaged in the years before turning to Michael Wayne to run his financial affairs. After starting to do commercials for Datril and Great Western Savings, he told me one of his friends asked him why John Wayne would go on TV and peddle aspirin.

"The truth is, Aissa," he said, "I'm doing it for the money. I'm not broke or anything like that, but I've spent too much, and trusted too many people. If Michael had been old enough to manage my money from the start, I'd never have had these problems. You've gotta find something you can fall back on, Aissa. If I get sick, I don't know what will happen to you kids. It's not what you think it is, Aissa."

My second year at USC I was put on an allowance of $200 a month. Though barely getting by, I was reluctant to ask for more. For two reasons: I was striving for my independence, and by then, asking my dad for extra cash was to court a three-minute discourse on frugality. One night that semester, I walked into his house and he handed me an already-opened envelope. My father said, "Here, it's a three-hundred-dollar dentist bill. Pay it. You're making your choices now. Start paying your own bills."

Too childlike to understand he was trying to teach me responsibility, I actually felt unloved. "I can't believe it," I whined to Debbie. "I'm still in school and my father is making me pay my own bills."

That summer I tagged along with my mom when she began real estate school. I quickly discovered I not only understood them, I was fascinated by how these transactions worked. As home values went rocketing, knowing that agents across Orange County were getting rich didn't hurt either. Seeking financial freedom, I made a choice, as my father had fifty years before, to drop out of college and enter the work force. The dilemma was, how do I break it to him?

I didn't, not yet. I waited instead until I finished the real estate course and passed the exam and knew I'd be granted my license. I didn't inform my dad of my fait accompli until just two weeks before USC fall classes.

He was offended: I'd taken the course on the sly. "If you love me," he'd always say, "then I'm not the last to know. If you love me you'll tell me things first."

He was displeased: his daughter would not earn her college degree.

But then he quieted down and looked me dead in the eye and saw something new there—determination. He spoke the basic words I waited a long time to hear.

"You started something," he said, "and you saw it through. Now you have something that's yours. I wish you all the success in the world. I've never been prouder of you."

After *that,* I stopped by his house every day, to tell him about new listings, new escrows, a newly learned trick of the trade. "Aissa," he said one early morning, "say hello, how are you."

"What?"

"Say hello, how are you."

"Hello, how are you?" I said in a girlish voice.

"No, no, no," he corrected. "If you're going to sell real estate, you can't talk like that anymore, that voice. You have to say, 'Hello! How are you?' You have to be a businesswoman now."

We went back and forth—"Hello! How are you?"—but it didn't strike me until I was alone that night. With my friends and my clients, I did speak assertively. Only my father could still make me feel ten years old.

That I was twenty and selling real estate did not make me unique in 1970s Newport Beach. That my father was John Wayne did. No longer embarrassed about my last name, and now having my own mortgage to pay, I put my name to good use, earning enough that first year to purchase a one-bedroom home in nearby Costa Mesa. My father, the expert on everything, would often drive over and tell me where to position my sofa, the value of planting perennials—except now his lectures were cherished. I felt so proud that he liked my new little house.

One night that summer we barbecued outside, just he and I in the Bayshores backyard. It was a warm and gently breezy Pacific night, and as we chatted and ate and admired the copper sky, he shifted his gaze from the afterglow to me.

"I know that you really love me," he said. "I know you've always loved me, Aissa."

All my words went away. I couldn't speak, but knew I didn't have to. What I felt was filling my eyes.

After that perfect night, in that special summer, when my father stopped demanding my love, most of my fear of him dissolved. For the last five years of his life, when I told my father "I love you," I did not mean, "See, Dad, I'm bucking you up again." When he said he loved me, he did not seem to mean, "Now you must tell me back, and tell me again and again, because today I am feeling weak." I still lament that it took so long, that we both played so fast and loose with our time together in life, and yet when my father died, our relationship was closer, stronger, less panicked than I'd ever dreamt it could be. I think he approved of me when he left, and saw without my words how much his love meant. I'll always have certain regrets, but our resolution has left me feeling blessed.

29

I n the new winter of 1976, I flew to Nevada to visit my
dad, who was making *The Shootist* with Jimmy Stewart, Lauren Bacall, and Ronnie Howard. In light of his
health, I was nearly sure it would be his final movie.

As much as he admired Jimmy Stewart and Lauren
Bacall, I think my father enjoyed Ronnie Howard most of all.
He always said Ronnie was the most talented young actor
he'd ever worked with, a pretty big compliment coming from
a man whose career spanned fifty years. Until very near his
death, my father clung to the dream of making a script called
Candy's Man. Whenever he spoke of it, he always said he
wanted to make it with Ronnie Howard.

His affection for his costars notwithstanding, making
The Shootist was a gloomy experience. Prior to filming my

father contracted pneumonia, and was shorter of breath than I'd seen him in many years. Several mornings before he could start work, we had to lay him face down across a table, where a physical therapist pounded my father's back to try and dislodge the fluid clogging his lung.

The Shootist, I felt, was a solid picture, richer and more compelling than anything my father had done since *True Grit.* It felt just right, my dad going out with a Western.

Still, when the film was complete I found I could barely watch it. John Bernard Books, his character, is a legendary gunfighter coming to terms with his death. I had watched my father die in seven other movies. But he always died for a cause, usually noble. In this film he was dying of cancer, and that was extremely unnerving. If not quite a family curse, for us the spectre of cancer had never entirely faded. By the time of *The Shootist,* the disease had killed my Uncle Bob, and I'd lived ever since with the fear that cancer would come again for my dad. Though his cancer would not be diagnosed for two more years, when he made *The Shootist* I think my father had similar apprehensions. When *The Shootist* came out, what I saw on-screen in my father's eyes did not seem to be acting. The loneliness there looked real.

From *The Shootist* on, he was almost continuously sick. By March 1978, even his voice was failing, a condition my father hated even more than his wheezing or dizziness; without his voice he could not continue working. For a while he tried hiding it, refusing interviews with press, speaking only to those who were not in the business of making movies. When he finally saw a doctor, a defective valve was discovered inside his heart. Evidently due to all his violent coughing, he'd ripped a "string" in his mitral valve, which controls the flow of blood between the left atrium and and the left ventricle of the heart. The cardiologist said this was actually decent news: rather than a generally failing heart, my father had a single, isolated, correctible flaw. A successful operation, they said, could return his heart to full strength.

But, my father was not a young or healthy man. Seventy years old, his weight had ballooned to the range of 250. The doctors feared he might not be well enough to survive the trauma of open-heart surgery, and my father was also reluctant, albeit for typically bullheaded reasons. He was determined to star in *Candy's Man,* and to fulfill his commercial obligation to Great Western Savings. For the time, in the hope of getting by despite his damaged valve, he would only agree to take medication.

That hope was ruined one night in March 1978, when I stepped outside my old bedroom. In the same hall he once paced after fights with my mom, my father stood motionless, his sturdy head bowed.

"I'm so dizzy," he said. "Aissa, I don't know what is happening to me."

An angiogram, a heart X ray projecting a clear picture of the cardiac area, provided the answer. His mitral valve *must* be replaced, and it must be done promptly. On March 29, 1978, accompanied by my father, Michael and Patrick Wayne, and Pat Stacy, I flew to Boston, where specialists at Massachusetts General Hospital would replace my father's valve with one from the heart of a pig.

On the private plane ride east my father mostly napped. When he awoke, there were plenty of oinking and pig jokes. "Make sure I don't have a curly tail when they bring me out of surgery," my father cracked. "Don't worry about me. I'll still be able to oink with the best of them." Always considered "the serious one," I could never see the black humor in sickness the way my father and his older kids could. I never especially liked that about myself. But that's who I was, and I felt too fearful now to even feign laughter.

Upon first inspection, the Eastern hospital only deepened the chill I'd felt from the instant I'd heard my father's heart was not right. Used to the bright, pastel, wall-papered hospitals of Southern California, I was anxious about the dismal brown corridors and faded tile floors of Massachusetts General. My father's spartan room had an iron bed, a chair, a nightstand, a closet, and no air conditioning. At first I felt horrendously depressed: this is a place where people come to die.

It was, in fact, a marvelous place, where wonderful doctors help people keep living. Unlike UCLA, which had all the proper cosmetics, and where my father's doctors were cold and obtuse, his Boston doctors were direct, friendly and patient. Contrary to UCLA, where, later, no one ever said, This is how cancer works, this is where it is now in your dad, this is where we hope it doesn't spread, the Boston doctors detailed every stage of the coming ordeal. Using the valve of a pig, they explained, sounded peculiar but was widely considered the safest and most efficient procedure. The critical juncture would come about ninety minutes into the three-hour operation. My father's heart would then be removed from his chest and placed on a pump while the doctors switched valves. When his heart came back off the pump, it was crucial that it resume beating. Due to my father's age and chronic bronchitis, the risk factor was roughly 10 percent. Dr. Roman DeSanctis, the serene, devoted lung specialist, and Dr. Mortimer Buckley, the tall, elegant heart surgeon, said we had every reason to be optimistic.

The night before surgery, DeSanctis and Buckley allowed my father to join us for dinner. By then all my brothers and sisters and a few of my father's close friends had flown east. My mother stayed in Newport, waiting for my phone calls. By that point in their lives, both she and my dad had agreed he was too physically weak to withstand the emotional strain of even trying to get back together. The rest of us met in a private room at Maison Robert, a restaurant in old Boston, taking our seats as my father assumed his place at the head of the table. To no one's surprise he ordered a drink. When we protested he argued, until one of my brothers left the room to phone the doctors. The verdict returned— he could have one drink but no more—my father ordered the "largest martini your bartender can make. That's one drink, isn't it?" There was a lot of clearing of throats but nobody spoke. With this crowd the Duke was still the boss.

The waiter brought it out in a wine glass. Swishing around his martini, my father rose and toasted his family and friends. "To the last supper," he said, and then he winked. He was referring to the churchlike decor of the room, its stained glass windows and heavy wooden tables. But of course we all saw through him. As it had all of ours, my father's death had been crossing his mind.

The next morning, exactly as promised, Dr. DeSanctis entered our crowded room about ninety minutes into my father's surgery. DeSanctis entered holding his thumb straight up, sparing us that agonizing instant when families must try and decipher their doctor's vacant expression. "The heart came off the pump perfectly," DeSanctis said. "Everything's going fine. Your father should be fine." I ran to a phone and called my mother in California, grinning so broadly I looked like another girl. My rock of a dad was alive. He'd defeated open-heart surgery, just as so many years ago he'd vanquished cancer.

Despite being forewarned by Dr. DeSanctis, I was humbled and shaken when I saw my dad that afternoon. Wired up, strapped down, a respiratory tube running gruesomely into his swollen throat, he looked bleached and battered, and the tubing kept him from speaking although he was awake. I wanted to squeeze him, but did not even touch him for fear of touching too hard.

30

W as I like the rest of his fans, mesmerized by his image? Or was my father truly larger than life? He was, in fact, an incredible man. Before we left Boston, Dr. DeSanctis told my dad he could live another fifteen years with his new, improved heart. If my father did not believe, he wasn't showing it. Back only weeks in Newport, he purchased several pairs of new cotton sweat clothes and a new cushy pair of gleaming white gym shoes. Every morning at six, he walked a slow one-mile lap around the complex at Bayshores. A few mornings a week I dragged myself out of bed and strolled the one mile with him, my dad telling me stories, saying hello to fellow habitual walkers, noting changes in his neighbor's familiar homes.

"See those begonias," he'd say to me. "See how much they've perked up the front of that house?"

I enjoyed those lazy walks, and for all my concern I had to confess he looked good, fantastic really, for a seventy-year-old guy who'd just endured open-heart surgery. Having shed thirty pounds he didn't want or need, his stamina returned, his dizzy spells passed, and even his voice returned to normal.

Why then was my father so irate?

And he *was* irate. No sooner would we conclude our morning walks than he would commence attacking "those dirty bastards." In the past, when he railed at the liberal press and politicians, I never felt too threatened, not even those two or three times he hurled objects through our TV sets. As long as he fumed at *The Washington Post* or Ted Kennedy, the heat was off of us and on someone else.

But this winter his tirades gave me the jitters. Who "those dirty bastards" were was not always clear, and often my father seemed mad at the "whole damn country." He was outraged at the talk of gun control, since criminals could still obtain firearms while law-abiding citizens went unprotected. He was sick about and appalled by Jim Jones and the mass death in Guyana. Most of all, he was disenchanted with the Carter administration. My father liked Jimmy Carter personally. Although my dad supported his old friend, Ronald Reagan, in 1976, when Carter won the election my father accepted his invitation to appear at the White House inaugural. In 1977, he even backed Carter on the Panama Canal, helping to push the new treaty through Congress. Through his relationship with Tony Arias, my godfather and his business partner before Mr. Arias's fatal plane crash, my father knew the Panamanians well. He said Panama had "sided with us in every international emergency since its existence. We made a commitment to Panama, and we must live up to it." This outraged my father's conservative fans, and put him at odds with Ronald Reagan, but my father stood firm. For all his blustery ways, he always said he prided himself on looking at issues one by one.

By 1978, though, despite that he'd just been allied with Carter one year ago, my father was calling him an "uninspiring leader, an ineffectual president." As long as Carter remained in the White House, my father predicted that winter, Americans would continue losing their confidence, our economy would stay in its tailspin, and this country would be emasculated even more as a world power. "The United States is losing its balls and its spirit," my father said. "It's gotten so crappy here, I can't stand to see it."

One afternoon at his house, my father said he was leaving. Speaking quietly, but with conviction, he told me he was moving to Mexico.

"I have no reason to stay here. Your mother and I are busted up. The Mexican people love me, and I'm damn near about to give up on the USA. I'll get a house, I'll get a smaller boat. You can come down and stay with me. All the children can. There's nothing quite like Baja."

Initially I simply didn't believe him. I knew he adored it down there, both the countryside and the Mexican people, especially Latin women. I knew he was frustrated and angry with the illnesses that plagued him for nearly three years. I also knew my father defied easy labeling, was not the two-dimensional man the myth machine had long made him out to be (often with his cooperation). However brash, a move to Mexico wasn't beyond my dad.

And I still didn't believe him.

I was sure he'd continue regaining his health, feel more positive toward his own self, and reembrace the country I knew he still fervently loved beneath his cynical words.

Later, first slowly and then in a flood, I started developing doubt. He certainly appeared serious. In preparation for the move, he began taking Spanish lessons, for the first time in his life, although all three of his wives had been Latin. Three times weekly, his tutor drove to the house and they'd huddle at the small table in the kitchen where Fausto ate his meals. I'd go over and see him, my father playing student, and I'd roll my eyes and he'd chuckle. For once, I thought with some pleasure, he cannot overshadow me. With a

Peruvian mother and two Peruvian maids, I'd spoken Spanish fluently for years. My father sounded like . . . John Wayne speaking Spanish.

Though we never discussed potential reverberations, surely he knew they'd be great. *U.S. News and World Report* once wrote that John Wayne symbolized "the virtues and strengths that Americans like to believe are typical of their country." It's one thing for an elderly icon to criticize his troubled country. But had my father really become an expatriate—and told the world why—the shock waves might have been global.

For six months my father dutifully took his lessons, insisting that after the Oscars, after making *Candy's Man,* he was packing his rods and reels and heading south for Baja's rugged grandeur. Neither one of us ever found out if he'd back up his words. Cancer robbed my father's bittersweet dream.

31

I t happened on one of our morning walks. Hands clutching his stomach, abdominal pain etched on his face, in
midstride my father doubled over. When he straight-
ened back out he said he was fine, but later that week
the burn in his stomach returned and my father con-
sulted a doctor. A biopsy was taken. The doctors said there
were no signs of cancer.

When my dad resumed his walks, the razor-sharp pain
froze him in place again, again while I was with him. Later,
back at the house, he told me it felt like jagged glass had been
raked against the inside of his stomach.

"Aissa," he said softly. "I know I have the Big C again."

"It can't be. They did biopsies. You don't have the Big C.
I know you don't."

"I have it, Aissa. I feel it inside my body."

I was not telling my dad what I thought he wanted to hear. Since the doctors spotted no cancer, I thought his discomfort was coming from something else. Later, I learned that certain types of cancer cells can hide out, and my father's had hidden deep inside the lining of his stomach. When at last they discovered it, the doctors said my father's cancer was very slow and might have been inside him for months or even years. When first I heard this notion it made me physically ill. As it sank in—cancer might have been killing him, gradually, and nobody knew it—my squeamishness turned to a kind of hatred. Not at the doctors, but hatred at cancer itself, a fickle, cunning disease with phony retreats that foster hope, followed by brutal frontal advances. With cancer, I learned, no one ever really feels certain. Not patients, not family, not even superstar doctors.

By December my father could not stand the smell of most food and mostly ate fruit. He began dropping weight and the doctors urged further exploratory surgery. But Christmas was near, the holiday he so loved, and my dad insisted on being at home with family and friends. As he did every Christmas Eve, he invited a pair of Newport Beach couples, the DeFrancos and the Reafsnyders, to the Bayshores house for dinner. Most Christmas Eves the women cooked and sipped champagne while the men drank liquor and gabbed about sports and politics. This night, my father could not make it through our meal. Excusing himself, he fled the scent of liquor and food and went to lie down. By then, around me, he'd stopped concealing his weakness, but was still professing decent health around his friends. At this revealing moment, it hit me hard just how sick my father felt— too sick to pretend. As the Reafsnyders and DeFrancos left early, I wondered if he'd make it until the following Christmas.

Two weeks later, Barbara Walters arrived at the Bayshores house to interview my dad for one of her prime-time ABC specials. I was struck by how pretty she looked off-camera, and how genuine she seemed. Though weakening day by day, my father had made the deal with Miss Walters's office several months earlier, and he was determined to honor it. Miss Walters didn't know, since no one told her, he would start taking tests for cancer the very next morning.

At one point in their talk my father did say he'd be hospitalized the following day, but he owed it to gall bladder trouble. In truth, gallstones had once been discussed as the possible problem, but the theory had been discarded. By then we all feared he had cancer. My father himself told his doctors, "Get rid of anything you find. I don't care what you have to do. Get it out." The gall bladder story, one we'd all been instructed to stick to, was contrived for the press. I could see my father started liking Barbara Walters the moment he met her; I could also see how uneasy he felt at leading her on.

If he did have cancer again, the doctors had two prevailing theories. It might have been triggered by his heart surgery, since such a radical jolt to the system can sometimes enliven previously dormant cells. Or it might have been all that hot smoke, passing through my father's lungs and into his stomach. When I heard *that,* I felt a pang in my own insides. It makes no difference, remember, how long or how much a person has smoked: the moment they stop they reduce their chances for cancer. But my dad, even after losing one lung to cancer in 1964, had not quit smoking. Oh, he stopped smoking Camels, but first he started chewing tobacco, then he infrequently smoked cigars, then he was smoking cigars all the time.

"I'm not inhaling," he always said, but he was and all of us knew it. I, for one, never made any real effort to stop him. I dropped a few benign hints but I never said, "I don't want to lose you—why can't you stop?" My reluctance came partly from fear and deference, partly because I was smoking myself by the time I entered high school. I smoked behind my parents' backs, with my girlfriends, struggling to look cool and adult, coughing my brains out, then drowning the scent of Virginia Slims with gum and Binaca. Who knows? Perhaps I was also emulating my father, self-ruinous habits and all.

It's one more reason I'll always feel some sorrow that I was afraid of him for so many years. Had I been less hesitant, we might have been free all that time to discuss meaningful things. I'll never know, but maybe I could have pushed him to give up his cigars. My mother tried to when she quit smoking and drinking herself when we moved to Newport. My father said no, but at least she gave it an honest shot. I just sat there watching him smoke.

32

January 10, 1979, my father entered UCLA Medical Center, located on the college campus in Westwood. The smokescreen was already erected: since he was in fine physical shape, since he had no immediate obligations, John Wayne decided this was the perfect time to treat a chronic gall bladder problem.

After two days of tests the doctors operated, strongly supposing they'd locate the cancer once they cut inside the inner stomach. For three hours we waited without a word in our ninth-floor room at UCLA. It was almost noon when the doctor appeared. "I want the Wayne family," he said, "just the Wayne family, please."

No, I thought, it can't be. My father is not dead. Through

the haze in my brain I heard someone say, "What is it? What is it?"

The doctor, his face a hard blank slate, did not reply, only gestured to the door, and I felt my hostility rising. Going in, my father had been so weak . . . it was such a grueling delicate operation . . . just say it, damn it. Tell us if he has cancer. Tell us if he survived.

By the time the doctor led us out of the waiting room, down the corridor, into my father's private room, I had convinced myself the dreaded moment had come. My father's death. We had not even said goodbye.

"Well," said the brilliant, icy physician, "our suspicions were correct. Mr. Wayne does have a carcinoma. We have no option but to remove the entire stomach . . ."

After that the doctor said a few more words, but all I heard was murmuring. My father had cancer. He would learn he lost his stomach when he woke up. He'd given the doctors that right, but that would not blunt his horror.

That dreary afternoon the hours lagged on and on and carried us numbly into the night. While his stomach was removed, and a substitute stomach fashioned from his intestines, my father remained in surgery for another six hours. Meanwhile, our phony gall bladder story completely backfired. First told that John Wayne's operation was purely routine, somehow that night the press learned my father was still in surgery. As print and electronic media inundated UCLA, two colossal tabloid idiots even tried photographing my dad while he lay on the operating table. Somehow, they bypassed security and donned a pair of white lab coats. Hiding their camera, they tried sneaking up to the operating chamber. They were detected before they got in, but we were all furious. How recklessly perverse could the supermarket press get?

Nine hours after they took my father in, *nine hours,* his doctor resurfaced. They'd excised all the cancer they found, but could not confirm that they'd spotted it all. They would have to continue the biopsies. For now, though, my father was in "satisfactory condition."

Even in my agony, I felt it was a beginning.

I didn't know it was also a finish in some way for me. Because from that conversation on, until my father died five months later, my direct contact with his doctors at UCLA was practically nonexistent. Every finding they made, they reported only to Michael Wayne, my forty-five-year-old half brother. Evidently, he and the doctors had forged a private agreement: they'd talk to him, and he'd inform the other six children. I knew we were a large and unwieldy group, and that doctors are busy people. But our Boston group was big, too, and the Mass General doctors were also stretched thin. At this pressing stage of my father's life, I wanted to hear about his cancer, his good turns as well as bad, from experts and not secondhand. Though the process burned me up, for many weeks I stifled myself and said nothing. At twenty-three years old, I was still sufficiently passive, still intimidated enough by my father's oldest son, Michael, to outwardly accept what inwardly enraged me.

In future weeks, taking shifts by our father's bedside, we all became punchy and exhausted. As the inexorability of his death dangled above us, instead of dealing with our stress, fear, and grief in even a semiopen, seminurturing way, the doctors and Michael kept meeting privately, the flow of information grew more and more muddled, and the tension between us mounted. From what I've learned since, we were a classic example of how families should not deal with cancer.

I should have expected to hear it this way, but I wasn't prepared when I did. Three days after the operation, while driving back to UCLA, I jabbed a button on my dashboard and a man on all-news radio detailed the local stories. He said an announcement was issued that morning by a UCLA Medical Center spokesman: "More cancer has been found in actor John Wayne. Lab tests show the cancer has metastasized into his gastric lymph nodes."

My long deep breaths didn't help. I had to clench the

wheel to remain inside my lane. *Metastasized* is the bleakest word in the medical language of cancer. It meant my father's had spread; his surgeons had not found it all. Of course it was nobody's fault, but hearing it like this—in my car, on the radio, a report on my dad segueing into stocks, weather, and traffic—filled me at first with murderous indignation. They could not tell the whole family, first, before they went public? And who were "they" anyway? Who exactly was making these choices?

By a mile or so later my brain stopped screaming. My thoughts turned back to my father, what this new development meant to him. With radiation or chemotherapy, lymphatic cancer sometimes goes into remission. But far more often lymphatic cancer is fatal.

I drifted through traffic crying.

33

By Valentine's Day my dad was back home but too sick to eat much, and what he could ingest he could not keep down. As his weight dropped all the way to 170 pounds, his face became so gaunt I saw features to it I never knew existed. His upper body, once so robust, lay withered and wasted, deflated to half its normal size. By that Valentine's Day, only my father's eyes had not betrayed him. With his face shrunken they looked even bigger, and they still shone clear and calm and resolute. Even when I was deeply depressed, I could still lose myself for a time in his incandescent blue eyes. In my father's eyes, I could still see the same strong man who strode through my childhood.

That winter, my father received few visitors. Pat Stacy was often around, and for that I was grateful. My father, remember, had a weakness few people knew about: he could not bear to be alone. By then, my mother was keeping her distance, not wanting to burden my dad, but also unsure of what his relationship with Pat had become. At this lonely time in his life, he and my mother spoke only on the phone, and even then only rarely.

That winter I went to his house nearly every day. And despite his departing flesh, my father's spirit slowly started advancing. Though he no longer spoke of Mexico, he vowed to get well, to begin radiation, to go to the Oscars that spring, and to resume his career that summer. By then I'd seen his X rays' blackened shadows, and yet when I heard him make these pronouncements, I found myself believing. My father had taken a stand, and once he took a stand it was always extremely hard to get him to yield it.

As spring neared he spent less time inside and more outside on the patio, basking in the sun and ocean air, gearing up for April's Oscars, which by then had become my father's holy grail. Early that March, rumors of John Wayne's imminent death had swept through Hollywood. One day he read an item about himself in the morning paper, and when I came over that afternoon he was sitting outside in his favorite spot, staring across the bay at the Newport Harbor Yacht Club. "I'll show those SOBs," my father said, hellbent. "Those bastards think I'm dying. Nothing is happening to me!"

On Monday, April 9, I did not accompany him to the Academy Awards. There was a shortage of tickets that year for presenters, and my father had promised Marisa, who'd only been three when he won for *True Grit,* that one day he'd take her with him to the Oscars. Perhaps he believed this would be his last chance.

The afternoon of the show I stopped in at my father's suite at the Bonaventure Hotel, a short drive from the Music Center in downtown Los Angeles, the venue for that night's telecast. To appear less emaciated, by then he'd begun wearing loose-fitting clothes around the house and extra layers of clothing the few times he went out in public. For the Oscars, he had ordered a smaller tuxedo, but kept losing weight in the interim. That afternoon, his new tux already too large, he put on a wet suit beneath it to make himself look heavier.

Along with his weight, he felt anxious about the best picture award he'd been chosen to present. He did not want to mangle names, which even at his best my father was prone to do. He was most concerned about Warren Beatty, the producer-star of *Heaven Can Wait.* Warren Beatty, my father said, hated it when people called him Warren *Beety.* Determined to say it correctly, my father practiced again and again in the mirror: "Warren *Beatty.* Warren *Beatty.* Warren *Beatty.*"

Late that afternoon I drove back to Newport alone to make it home in time for the show, but a part of me was hoping my dad would decide on a last-minute cancellation. For all I knew this night meant to him, when I left him he looked peaked. For several weeks he'd had trouble merely standing for any extended duration, and now he was sick and the Oscars was such a long show and best picture award always came at the very end. I was scared he might be exhausted by then, walk out, and collapse on national TV. Even if he recovered, I knew what that would do to my father's pride.

My father, of course, showed up, and by then I had changed my mind. He'd been so dead set on making this engagement, to miss it now could debilitate him even more than sticking it out could. That evening I watched the awards on TV with a handful of friends, and the show ran long as usual. Finally, the producers ran a clip of Bob Hope, pulled from the Oscar one year before, when my father was bedridden at Massachusetts General.

"Duke, we miss you tonight," Bob Hope said. "We expect to see you amble out here in person next year, because nobody else can walk in John Wayne's boots."

From the image of Mr. Hope, the camera swung back to Johnny Carson, this evening's emcee. "Ladies, Gentleman," Johnny Carson said, "Mr. John Wayne."

By the time my father reached the Music Center stage,

the industry crowd rose as one and its standing ovation swelled to a human crescendo. They clapped so heartfelt and long—for the voice, the walk, the classic lines and scenes, his bravery and his will—my father could not start his speech. Watching at home I barely breathed. Pride welled in my throat, and my heart said, *Keep on clapping forever, let it wash over him, he needs your love, it will give him strength.* But my rational mind said, *Stop, he can't stand up, stop and let him get off, can't you see he's not going to make it?*

The camera panned the seats as the Hollywood people cried. My own tears came as they zoomed back in for another close-up. He was perspiring now, and he looked so deathly thin. It was like watching him walk a tightrope.

When the clapping finally died, my father spoke in a shaking voice: "That's just about the only medicine a fella'd ever really need. Believe me when I tell you that I'm mighty pleased that I can amble down here tonight. Oscar and I have something in common. Oscar came to the Hollywood scene in 1928—so did I. We're both a little weatherbeaten, but we're still here, and plan to be around a whole lot longer. My job here tonight is to identify your five choices for the outstanding picture of the year and announce the winner, so let's move 'em out."

My father kept on, announcing the nominees, and then he came to Warren Beatty. And my father could not say it right. Still, even then, John Wayne got it wrong uniquely: he didn't stumble on Beatty, but my father called him "Warner." I let out a nervous laugh and one of my girlfriends said, "What?" I was so absorbed in my father I'd forgotten I wasn't alone.

The Deer Hunter won best picture, and when my dad presented the Oscar to its director, Michael Cimino, he called him Michael "Camino." I cried and laughed then, too, but when it was over a few mispronounced names meant nothing at all, except perhaps to my stubborn dad. For the rest of us watching that indelible night, I think we all felt honored

and moved, and that we had all shared in something re-
soundingly special. It was his final appearance in public,
John Wayne's last public battle. I won't say he won—he was
still dying of cancer—but, oh, what a fight my courageous
father put up.

34

S omething is wrong with me, Aissa. Something is really wrong."

Three weeks after bidding the public farewell, my father keeled over next to his kitchen stove. The calendar said May 2, 1970, and that night we would rush him to not one, but two different hospitals. My dad never came home again.

We took him first to Hoag Hospital in Newport Beach, where X rays revealed an intestinal blockage. His doctor at Hoag instructed us to drive him to UCLA, for an emergency surgery the following morning. My father's pain was so severe he couldn't sit up, so we folded down his station wagon's back seat, spread out some blankets, and laid him gently back there. Ethan drove the wagon and Marisa and I followed him in my car. As we pulled into UCLA, I could not see the emergency entrance for all the camera equipment and bodies. In the short time since we'd left Hoag, someone had tipped off the press.

Mimicking Ethan's U-turn, I sped behind him around the near corner, screeching to a stop at the hospital's back-side. Still bent over, my father came out of the wagon curs-ing. "That chickenshit nurse at Hoag, I know she was the one. How dare she degrade me like this. I know that son of a bitch called the press."

After two guards snuck him in through a service en-trance, he was admitted into his room. Thinking it might calm him down, we pressed on the TV. Platinum-haired Jerry Dunphy, a longtime local newsman whom my father counted a friend, was informing greater Los Angeles County that John Wayne had been rushed to UCLA for unknown reasons. In seconds my dad was on the phone to ABC, and five minutes after the newscast Dunphy returned the call.

"You bastard!" my father screamed. "I thought you were a friend! You put me on the news five minutes after I check in? Goddamn it, Jerry! Now I won't have a moment's peace."

Sadly, my father was right, though not solely for the reasons he meant. Wednesday morning, surgeons removed a large part of his colon: new cancerous cells were found in the excised tissue. Further tests showed the cells had multiplied and spread throughout my father's body. The radiation treat-ments hadn't worked.

Once UCLA released its findings, it was bombarded by phone calls and visitors. Most were screened or turned away by Pat Stacy, on orders from Michael Wayne, who in turn had conferred with the doctors. I understood their reasoning: though all of his callers and visitors meant well, what little strength my father had left he needed to hoard to fight off the cancer. What I never understood was the rhyme or reason behind who did and who didn't get in. Joe DeFranco, Barry Goldwater, James Bacon, all old friends of my father, were refused entry when they tried seeing him. Henry Fonda only said good-bye to my dad because he swore he would sit at the hospital all night, and even talk to the doctors if that's what it took. Frank Sinatra, meanwhile, was deemed a suitable guest, despite that he and my father had never been close.

Although it was no real fault of his own, I found Mr. Sinatra's visit especially upsetting. The day he arrived with his wife, my father wasn't prepared yet to see them, so Barbara and Frank chatted with us in the waiting room next door. Mr. Sinatra was upbeat, and definitely "on."

"Nice to meet ya," he said. "How you doin'? You know, I haven't seen your dad in a while."

When told my father was ready, the Sinatras stepped next door into room 948. When they returned to our room a few minutes later, Sinatra the performer had been replaced by a shaken man with tears in his eyes.

"I am so sorry," he said. "I had no idea your father was that sick. If there's anything I can do . . ."

His shock and emotion were real, and that's what frightened me. Having been near my father's side day after day after day, his ravaged appearance no longer seemed peculiar. Mr. Sinatra's reaction recalled a lingering fact I still preferred denying.

I suppose guilt is always a potent sensation, but perhaps never more than when someone we love faces death. I cannot say when my own guilt feelings ended, or if to this day they entirely have, yet I precisely recall their beginnings. After my father's radiation failed, the doctors tried immunotherapy, a fairly new treatment in which chemicals were injected into his body in the hopes of stimulating his immune system. Waiting to hear the results of the treatment one morning, I thought Pat Stacy said the immunotherapy had slowed the advance of my father's cancerous cells. With cancer, sometimes you feel like nothing is being done, that the cancer just keeps creeping. This was the best news I'd heard in several weeks. Brimming with new inspiration, I rushed into see my father. He looked like he'd just been dozing.

"Dad," I said softly, "I'm glad you're improving. I'm so glad you're feeling a little bit better."

His blue eyes opened slightly wider, and then he closed them and went back to sleep smiling.

That afternoon, Michael Wayne pulled me aside.

"Did you tell him he was getting better? Where do you get off giving him that information?"

"I heard it, from Pat. Isn't he?"

"No! He's *not* getting better. You shouldn't have done that. You gave him false hope."

Michael was right. And after that rotten day, almost everything I did felt in some way inadequate. By then I'd moved into the Westwood Marquis Hotel, a few blocks from UCLA, and was seeing my father every day. Nevertheless, if Pat Stacy spent a night on the couch in the waiting room on my father's floor, I thought, *Why can't I be like her? She's there and I'm in my hotel room.* If I felt the urge to drive back home for one night, to briefly escape cancer wards and hotel rooms, the dejection and uncertainty ruling our lives, I also took this as proof that I was a shabby excuse for a daughter. I didn't know how to behave when someone I loved was dying. In my father's presence, I never knew what to confront and to avoid, what to feel and what to repress. Should I ever say the word *cancer*? Should I broach the chance of his death, family things he might wish me to do, when he had left them unmentioned? I understand now that many families dealing with cancer face similar problems, but in 1979 I did not. Mostly that final year I ate, and ate, and ate. While my father lost all interest in food for the first time in his life, I gained forty pounds. Since he couldn't eat, I'd touch nothing in front of him, then gorge myself when I was alone. God, was I screwed up.

By early June, we were all staying in shifts at UCLA, and the strain was also telling on Michael. If someone was five minutes late for a shift, Michael would chew them out, especially hard if the person late was my brother Ethan. One day I began hating it all—hating my fat, guilt-ridden self, hating my controlling brother Michael, hating the doctors who told me nothing, hating the cancer destroying my dad. When I returned that afternoon from lunch, Michael said, "Where the hell have you been?" I went crazy, shouting and crying and running to the elevator and right out the hospital door. I sprinted through campus until I found a bench, oblivious to the students striding in every direction around me. Just as my mind turned to them—Why do they look so young and full of purpose while my father is dying? Michael appeared as if out of nowhere.

"Get away from me," I said.

"Aissa."

"Get away from me. I can't take this anymore. I *have* to know what's happening."

"Look, I'm telling you everything. Nobody *knows* what's going on."

To an extent, I knew this was true. Even doctors can not predict cancer. But this anger had festered inside me ever since my father entered UCLA. All my life to that point, I had only heard Michael and my dad talk about money and business. I'd never once heard Michael ask my dad out to dinner, or to go to a ball game. Those final years in Newport Beach, we barely saw Michael at all. My father loved Michael Wayne and Michael loved him. But Michael knew it as well as I did: my father and I were always much closer, and even when things became strained during high school at least I was there. And yet now, after all those arms-length years, that was Michael's father in there, and not only I, but all the other children came second.

"Why can't we speak to the doctors?" I said.

Now Michael's manner was soothing. "I know how you feel," he said. "But there's eight people involved. And doctors and reporters and everyone else. We have to stay organized. Let me handle this thing."

"No! I demand to speak to the doctors!"

As Michael explained his side again I tuned him out, suddenly feeling so drowsy I felt I could nap right there on the bench. The summer sun felt mild and the manicured grass smelled freshly green. The campus was really a pretty place when you saw it from off that ninth floor. Just handle it all, big brother, I thought, feeling oddly drained. Go ahead and handle it all.

35

C ertain days my dad made life easy for his doctors, nurses, and attendants. More often, he fought them like a tiger. A man with a lifelong need for control, most of all he resisted his powerful drugs. Although he very much liked his nurses, he loathed their daily injections.

"Goddamn you," he said before almost every shot, "every time I turn around you're trying to stick me with that thing. Why are you sons of bitches giving me this shit? Do you want me so drugged up that I can't fight back? Jesus Christ!"

I took hope from my father's cantankerous outbursts. As long as he stayed defiant, it was hard not to feel he might somehow pull through. What's more, at that point my father was still intent on making his family feel secure, believing he must stay strong if the rest of us were not to lose our nerve. Still, I don't think it was all show. For all of his sickness and pain, my dad still seemed to appreciate his life. That May he would sit up in bed and look out his window and say, "What a lovely morning." He asked me all about Lornee, the man I was dating and my father's favorite backgammon partner. He questioned Marisa and Ethan on how they were doing at school. He still pointed to politicians on his TV: "Will you look at that son of a bitch? He's been telling the same lies so long, by now he believes them too!" What was funny about it then, the politician might be a Republican! When the cancer permitted, my father could still laugh and make others feel good, could still see the lightness in life.

Everything changed the first week of June. My father turned suddenly nervous and inward, his eyes darting and jumping at any movement or noise. That entire week, he could not focus for long on anyone or anything outside his own sick self. He even stopped hollering at his nurses. When they came in now with their Demerol and their morphine, they were no longer sons of bitches. Instead, he merely half-turned on his side and complied with their needles and pills. It broke my heart, and beneath their professional smiles I could see the nurses' hearts breaking too.

Up until this time, my father was still taking his daily walks, dragging his IV rack up and down the ninth-floor hall. Beneath his gown and USC cap, he had shrunk to little more than flesh and bone, and yet he still climbed from his bed every day for his three or four minutes, encouraging other patients, needling the nurses beside him, strolling just a little further, just a while longer on the strong days. One terrible morning his walks began shortening. A few days later, my father said he would take no walk at all.

"I'm just so fatigued," he explained, and I felt a great sadness and coldness. The following day, my father did not walk again and I knew he was ready to leave.

But the cancer wasn't willing to let him go. It would retreat for a day, perhaps two, and his doctors would issue more tests. On May 29, after X rays showed his intestines were almost entirely blocked, the doctors began him on intravenous morphine. After that, my father mostly floated. Late one afternoon I sat at his bedside, my father's mind drifting freely through time and place. With his eyes open wide, he said he had just returned from a wonderful parade. He said he marched in the middle of many majestic horses, and the drummers drummed and the streets were lined by children. I moved in closer to see if he was dreaming. No, his eyes stayed open. As he had more visions the following days, I was shocked that any drug on earth held the power to do this to my father. But at least the visions he nursed were always peaceful, and at least the morphine was keeping him warm.

As the morphine took hold, I also understood that a line had been crossed. Because for all the strides we'd made the past five years, emotional walls had sprung back up between us these final weeks. I wanted what I believed were simple things, and I wanted them intensely: to take him in my arms and tell my father I'd never forget him. That I hated that I could not help him. That he shouldn't worry, I would keep an eye on Marisa when he was gone. That I would lose all of this weight, and take care of myself again. So many things I needed to say.

And I wanted my father, as well, to confide in me, to admit he was scared of death, to tell me where it hurt, to ask would I please try and ease his suffering. None of this happened, because I knew he would not allow it, and because he was still my father. How he confronted his death could be his choice alone.

And yet still it all seemed so crazy. My father was dying and we were talking small talk. And then he was under the morphine, and then our time had run out.

So we never had that real talk, that sweet, sad summing up, and I never cried for my father where he could see me. One night close to the end, my girlfriend Debbie drove up from Newport Beach and we left UCLA for a nearby bar and a darkened booth and the numbing effects of a couple of drinks. Or so I had imagined.

"It will take your mind off things for a while," my old friend said, but after one glass of wine I felt my cheeks turning red and my throat closing up. Because Debbie would let me, because I couldn't stop, I cried and cried in the dark in her arms.

36

My father's life ended late in the afternoon of June 11, 1979. Three days before, he had slipped into and out of a coma. He remained in a coma the whole next morning and afternoon, then came out of it that evening at nine P.M. Until close to midnight, he was congenial and alert. And I alone was not there to see him.

Earlier that night, I'd kissed my sleeping father good-bye and driven back to Newport, to try and steal a decent night's sleep, to try and steel myself for the misery to come. Driving home, I realized I couldn't recall very much of our last conversation, except that my dad had asked about Lornee. Believing he'd never come out of his coma, it occurred to me that my father and I would never talk again.

Upon my return in the morning to UCLA, my brothers and sisters gave me the news from the night before. In bits and pieces, they all reported how fantastic it was to see him that way. For three hours, it was like having our old father back, they said. I smiled and said, "What a great thing," secretly wanting to know, Did he ask about me? Did he ask where I was?

How could I tell them how wretched I felt, how dishonorable? He was near death and once again I had failed him.

That Friday, my worst fear was that my father would die and I would be some other place, unable forever to say good-bye face to face. That morning, his third day in a coma, the doctors said he had less than twelve hours to live. All morning and afternoon I stayed upstairs. Shortly after five, Marisa and I rushed down to the cafeteria to eat what for us was lunch. The page came then. I ran to the phone and the voice at the other end said we'd better hurry right up, his blood pressure was plunging.

When we burst into the room he was still living, and his breathing was peaceful. It had become so tortured the past few days, I had feared my father might choke to death as he slept. Now he was breathing mildly, evenly, and except for Michael, who was with the lawyers, I think, we were all in my father's room—Patrick, Marisa, Melinda, Toni, Ethan, Pat Stacy, and myself. Moving in close I clasped his right hand. My father always had clean, attractive hands, and I noticed looking down that his hands still looked healthy—the cancer had not diminished them. As I held his hand, my father inhaled, and his breath never came back out.

My father died at 5:23 in the long summer daylight, encircled by six of his children. His passing should not have stunned me. He was seventy-two and had cancer. But it *did* stun me. The child within me believed he would live forever.

During my life I had never seen anyone die. And although my father went gently, it surprised me how quickly his life went when it did. One instant he was still breathing, still my dad—he died too fast. It was over too soon.

He really is gone, I thought, kissing his forehead. Moving

aside for the other children and Pat, I heard someone say, "He's in a better place now." It could be true, I said silently. He was so sick for so long. But it might not be true at all. He really liked living.

Brought back by all the hugging and sobbing, I started to worry for poor Marisa, only thirteen and crazy about her dad. "Make sure Marisa's okay," my father had said, the closest he'd come to addressing our lives after his death. I went to Marisa and held her, told her how much her daddy loved her, and about this time the nurse returned to draw the white sheet across my father's shoulders. "I love you, I'll miss you," I whispered, then with one look over my shoulder I crossed to the door.

"Don't cry, sweetheart," my mother said that night, sounding frail and far away. "It's a blessing. He's finally at peace."

37

According to Michael Wayne's plan, no outsiders could learn that our father had died yet.

To ensure his death not turn into a media sideshow, we were all told to conceal our grief, to pretend this was just another ordinary Friday. The facade went up even before we shuffled out of my father's ninth-floor room. Michael had hired a security guard to sit at the door and fend off the press and visitors, so we cleaned up our tears and nonchalantly walked out by the guard one at a time, smiling, saying, "See you in fifteen minutes," or "See you after lunch." Most of us then returned to the Westwood Marquis, where we checked out in staggered shifts to allay any suspicions.

"My sister and I are going home for the weekend," I told

the clerk, squeezing back tears, feeling like a liar and a fool. "We'll be back on Monday morning."

At the time it felt bizarre, but looking back I can see the flawless symmetry. The same day my father the Hollywood star died, I was still performing, sterilizing and masking my real feelings, concerned only with how things appeared.

Days before the funeral, I received phone calls from several friends and relatives. Had I seen the morning paper? My father, a news story alleged, had died a Catholic. He was baptized by a priest, according to the report, while he lay dying at UCLA. Knowing my father, how he felt about religion, I couldn't believe it.

I'd also been standing right there the alleged day. That morning, Michael Wayne said the Archbishop of Panama would be coming in to see our dad; there was no mention, to me, of any conversion. I knew my father had met the archbishop before, and that his relationship was warm with Panama's Catholic church. But friendship is one thing, religious belief entirely another. I knew firsthand how my father felt about Catholicism. I was raised a Catholic, and my father took no interest at all, never once attending church with me and my mom. Our entire lives, he showed no inclination toward organized religion of any type.

"I don't belong to any church," my father said. "I believe in God and Jesus Christ, and I pray. If anything, I guess I'm a Presby-goddamn-terian."

He said this with mischief in his voice, and it epitomized his offhanded feelings toward organized religion: more power to those who take it seriously, but I'm not one of them.

By the day the archbishop came to see him, my father was heavily drugged on intravenous morphine. He mostly drifted in and out of sleep, and even when awake not did appear coherent, but rather in some sort of dream state. When my father's eyes opened that day, the priest began reciting prayers in Latin. Under the bedcovers, I saw my father slightly nodding his head.

Was he converting to Catholicism on his death bed by this small movement of his head?

In my opinion, absolutely not. I believe he was only acknowledging that a priest was in his presence, and that they were praying together. My father never said a word about wanting to convert, or wanting to be buried instead of cremated. Frankly, I think he was too drugged up to know a conversion was even being attempted. It may comfort certain people to believe John Wayne died a Catholic, but I was a witness and I don't think so.

Remember, my father disliked funerals. Ward Bond's in particular had been sorrowful and drawn out, dismal and punishing for those in attendance. For himself, my dad preferred a memorial reflecting his life and his spirit. He asked to be cremated, and his ashes strewn over the channel between Newport Beach and Catalina Island. He so treasured that stretch of sea, it gave him so much peace during his lifetime, he wanted it for his final resting place. Fiercely superstitious, my father also heard tales of human scratching inside of caskets. "I want to be cremated," he said. "Just don't put me in a box." At their more sardonic moments, he and my mom used to joke that someone should slit their wrists after they "died." That way they *couldn't* be trapped alive.

After his ashes were scattered to sea, he wanted his family and friends to return to his Bayshores house for a lively Irish-style wake. "When I die," he told my mother more than once, "I want you to have a big party, and I want everyone to get DRUNK! Let everyone eat and drink and talk and remember the good times."

Unfortunately, he made no such provision in his will, and Michael Wayne made other arrangements. In the days after my father's demise, national tribute poured in from statesmen and entertainers, many of whom my father considered his friends, but none were invited to his funeral. Most of his friends, in fact, Hollywood or otherwise, were not invited to pay their respects. This included Joe DeFranco, my father's business associate and perhaps his closest friend at the time of his death.

Since everything was arranged in elaborate secrecy, even I wasn't informed of the funeral's time and setting until one day before. Only then did I learn that my father would not be cremated, but buried. He'd also receive no headstone, supposedly in the fear that his body could later be stolen by grave robbers. To keep things further obscured, the Catholic service would be held at 5:45 in the morning.

This whole thing stinks, I recall thinking. This is not the valedictory my father desired, or the one he remotely deserves. Let his old friends lavish him today with love and affection; allow them to miss him now, not just after he is gone; this is not the time to hoard him; this is when John Wayne should be shared; I hate it, all of it, and my father would hate it too.

All that, and still I mounted no protest. I told myself it was too late, there was no time, I was twenty-three years old and had never planned a funeral. Instead of even talking about it to Michael, I merely stood back and fumed, watching my father denied a fitting farewell. At that stage of my life, it was a classic Aissa Wayne nonreaction.

On June 15 I woke at four A.M., then drove half asleep to a Newport Beach church, where the same archbishop performed a Catholic service. The predawn gathering was small: the seven Wayne children, my mother, Pat Stacy, a few of my father's friends. Later, I rode to Pacific View Memorial Park, where the summer sun was contemplating rising over the graveyard. It's dawn, I said to myself, at least you'd like that, Dad—you always loved the dawn. Encased in a shiny coffin, my father's body was lowered into an unmarked grave. The words were said, the dirt shoveled over him. And then he was gone from my sight. My father. Into the earth. Fatherless now? That was all? Over so fast?

Chick Iverson came to me then. He said he had been a fine and big-hearted man. Together, Chick and I wept. His son, Chick Jr., lay in a grave only yards from where we stood. So much sadness in this life. I walked next to Chick from the grassy knoll out toward the gates and the cars. It was warm now but I was trembling.

Following the burial, my mother held a short and subdued and awkward reception. Even more so because of the funeral, which my mother knew my dad never wanted, her relations with Michael were strained. When most of the mourners had gone, I gazed at my mother across her dining room, recalling how much my father loved her. I remembered how he loved zipping her up as she dressed for a party, how on those Encino nights they always looked so young and carefree. I remembered their huge, safe, warm bed, and my climbing between them mornings when I was a child. "Three together," I used to say. "Three together always."

I felt a soft smile on my face for the first time that dark day.

My father was gone.

And would not be coming back.

But memories, I knew, wield a magic, a power, a comfort, a resiliency, all their own.

In memories, my father would always burn bright.

EPILOGUE

As my father's death crept closer, I often considered how I'd react when he was no longer around. I would be paralyzed by grief, I was fairly sure, unable to cope and perhaps unable to function. And then it came, my father's death, and my life was less than shattered. I lost weight, regained my healthfulness, and found a degree of success selling homes. For nearly two years, when I acknowledged my father's death at all, I felt hurt for Marisa, or Ethan, or my mom, while secretly feeling shame that my father's death had not done more to cripple me. For my father, for the public, had I subjugated my feelings so long that now I could no longer find them?

Whatever the causes, this numbness lasted nearly five

years. Then, although I recall no turning point, although I can't even tell you what triggered it, I was able to properly mourn. I admitted my father was gone, and how much that hurt, really, really hurt, and that this emptiness inside me would never completely fill back up. It was during this time, about five years after his death, when I first returned to my father's grave.

My mother had already been there several times, but I had refused all requests to join her. I did not really understand why I told my mother no, just as I didn't comprehend the stirring I felt that cool April morning to speak with my father. Amidst no crisis, there was nothing profound I felt I must say. And yet the impulse felt strong.

What was it?

I didn't know.

I let the feeling pull me where it wanted to go, to a corner store, where I purchased a bottle of liquor: Commemorativo tequila, his favorite. Arriving at the graveyard, I hurried past marble headstones, hunting for Chick Jr.'s grave, the signpost to my dad's. I found it and knelt on the moist morning ground above where my father lay. Over the grass now carpeting his grave, I poured the first shot for him; he always enjoyed tequila far more than I. Still, whatever this was, we were in it together. I downed a small cup myself. The brown liquor jolted my brain and burned my stomach. How could my father drink this? He always said he was only half-Irish, but I think he was *all* Irish. Was I talking outloud now or thinking? What was I doing here anyway? It was unnatural, to be drinking this way first thing, drinking tequila no less, among the dead at that. Still, for close to an hour I knelt there, sipping but mostly pouring. Talking to my father. Crying and laughing. Remembering. Forgiving. And understanding. The spring sun was heating the air and felt good on my arms. I did not want to leave him. Not yet. But I was feeling tipsy, and I still had to get back home. I knew there was just one solution. I sprinkled the rest of the liquor above him. Pictured him healthy and whole in my mind. Pictured my father smiling.

"I have to leave you now, Dad. But I'll come back soon. I love you. I know you love me. And wherever I go I'll take your love with me."

Then I stood up straight and started moving forward.

INDEX

Wayne, John (*cont'd*)
  patriotism of, 45–46
  in Peru, 12–14
  physical appearance of, 13, 26,
    54, 128–30, 195, 196–97
  politics of, 92–93, 103, 127–28,
    150, 151, 184–85
  and Otto Preminger, 97–98
  press on, 7, 9, 22–23, 36, 48–50,
    52–53, 54, 62–63, 72, 77,
    108–109, 113–14, 123, 127–28,
    134–36, 149, 173, 179, 188–89,
    192, 196, 201, 213
  as producer and director, 43–50
  production company of, 33–34,
    46–50, 73, 128
  in *Red River,* 76–77
  relationship with his brother, 16,
    17, 58, 104–106, 133
  relationship with his mother, 17,
    19, 37, 58, 105
  relationship with his son Ethan,
    154–56
  religion of, 71, 124, 214–15
  and Republic Pictures, 46
  resolution with Aissa, 177
  in *Sands of Iwo Jima,* 136
  sexual image of, 53–54, 141–43
  in *The Shootist,* 178–79
  and Frank Sinatra, 202
  singing of, 41–42
  smoking and coughing of, 48, 54,
    85, 98, 100–109, 124, 189–90
  in *The Sons of Katie Elder,*
    109–11, 113–14
  and Pat Stacy, 172–73, 195–96
  stunts performed by, 94–95, 113–14
  superstitions of, 14, 102, 215
  on television, 39, 61, 175, 180
  temper of, 55–56, 58, 59–60, 66,
    93–94, 125, 155, 165–66, 184,
    206, 207
  in *True Grit,* 128, 130–32, 135–38,
    196
  and Twentieth Century Fox,
    19–21, 53, 56, 74–75
  and United Artists, 46–50
  views on Hollywood, 20, 32–33,
    38–42, 79–80, 97–98, 132, 136
  weight problems of, 128–30, 179
  in Westerns, 4, 41, 43–50, 76–82,
    128, 179
  and *The Wild Goose* (yacht),
    83–90, 95, 112, 125
  and Grant Withers, 56
  and Darryl Zanuck, 73–75
Wayne, Marisa, 147, 154, 168, 196,
    200, 207, 208, 211, 212, 218
Wayne, Melinda, 23–25, 58, 211
Wayne, Michael, 23–25, 58, 73, 128,
    133, 173, 180
  and cancer of his father, 193,
    201, 203, 204
  and death of his father, 213–17
  Wayne's financial affairs run by,
    175, 204
Wayne, Patrick, 23–25, 58, 133, 180,
    211
  acting of, 47
Wayne, Pilar Palette, 12, 28, 64, 84
  in Africa, 76–82
  bed of, 123
  and birth of Aissa, 22, 23
  on boating trip to Europe (1963),
    84–96
  and cancer of her husband,
    100–109, 124, 190
  and death of Wayne, 212, 216,
    217, 219
  divorce from Wayne, 24, 167–70,
    173
  drug addiction of, 35–36
  fiestiness of, 34–35
  as a Hollywood wife, 32–36,
    67–68, 72, 123–24, 141–42
  independence of, 124–25
  marriage to Wayne, 8–9, 14–15,
    31–36, 72, 84–90, 93–98, 113,
    122–26, 129, 141–42, 154, 167,
    172–73, 181
  meets Wayne, 12–14
  miscarriages of, 72

ABOUT THE AUTHORS

AISSA WAYNE lives in Newport Beach, California.

STEVE DELSOHN is the co-author (with Jim Brown) of the national best-seller *Out of Bounds.* His work has appeared in *TV Guide, People, California,* and *Sport.*